CLIMATE CHANGE ADJUSTMENTS FOR DETAILED ENGINEERING DESIGN OF ROADS
EXPERIENCE FROM VIET NAM

JUNE 2020

ASIAN DEVELOPMENT BANK

Contents

Tables, Figures, and Boxes

Boxes

Acknowledgments

This knowledge product was planned and developed by the Climate Change and Disaster Risk Management Division, Sustainable Development and Climate Change Department (SDCC), of the Asian Development Bank (ADB), in close collaboration with ADB's Southeast Asia Department (SERD).

It was prepared by Robert Wilby, SDCC consultant, who also drafted the accompanying step-by-step manual. Both documents benefited from substantive input received from David Salter, principal natural resources and agriculture specialist, SERD; Charles Rodgers, SDCC consultant; and Xianfu Lu, former senior climate change specialist (climate change adaptation), SDCC. Support in their finalization was provided by Arghya Sinha Roy, senior climate change specialist (climate change adaptation), SDCC; Sugar Gonzales, climate change officer (climate change adaptation), SDCC; Mary Ann Asico, editorial consultant; and Edith Creus, layout artist.

Independent technical review by the following SDCC consultants is gratefully recognized: Clive Carpenter, Peter Droogers, Anthony Kiem, and Steven Wade.

This knowledge product and the step-by-step manual would also not have been developed without the encouragement and overall guidance of Preety Bhandari, chief of the Climate Change and Disaster Risk Management Thematic Group and concurrently director, Climate Change and Disaster Risk Management Division, SDCC.

Abbreviations

ADB	Asian Development Bank
BIIG	Basic Infrastructure for Inclusive Growth
CMIP5	Coupled Model Intercomparison Project, Phase 5
DED	detailed engineering design
GCM	general circulation model (or global climate model)
GEV	Generalized Extreme Value
IDF	intensity–duration–frequency
MONRE	Ministry of Natural Resources and Environment, Viet Nam
PPTA	project preparatory technical assistance
RCP	representative (greenhouse gas) concentration pathway
SLR	sea-level rise
TCVN	national standards issued by the Vietnam Standards and Quality Institute, Ministry of Science and Technology ("TCVN" stands for "Technical Committee of Vietnam")

Units of Measure

km	kilometer
km^2	square kilometer
m	meter
m^3/s	cubic meter per second
mm	millimeter
mm/y	millimeters per year
m/s	meter per second
m/y	meters per year
Rx1day	1-day annual maximum rainfall total

Executive Summary

Context

Climate change is expected to intensify heavy rainfall and raise global sea levels. Without adaptation and resilience measures, heavier rainfall and higher sea levels are likely to increase river and coastal flooding and erosion risk.

Economic analysis of adaptation options lies at the heart of the Asian Development Bank (ADB) project preparation phase. This involves the identification, then the valuation, of engineered and non-engineered adaptation options.

This knowledge product explains the rationale and procedures for incorporating allowances for climate change in detailed engineering design (DED). Attention is focused on credible adjustments to extreme rainfall and to mean and high-end sea-level rise, but the same principles and approaches could be extended to other design variables (such as extreme air temperature, evaporation, and wind speed).

Although climate hazards are treated separately here, it is important to recognize that these can occur at the same time: within the Asia and Pacific region, tropical cyclones bring heavy rainfall, with high wind speeds, waves, and storm surges. The DED should therefore reflect the possibility of climate-driven changes in *multi*-hazards at a site.

The procedures are demonstrated with worked examples drawn from the Viet Nam road transport sector and peer-reviewed research literature. An accompanying step-by-step manual shows how each calculation is performed. These principles and practices are intended to be transferable to other sectors, regions, and stages of the asset life cycle (from project concept to decommissioning).

Extreme Rainfall

Climate index severity, duration, and return period are typically mandated under national design standards for specified structures. In Viet Nam, national standards for roads and bridges require a design flood level of 1 in 100 years for expressways, and 1 in 25 years for category 3, 4, or 5 rural roads. The 1-day maximum rainfall total (Rx1day) is a critical variable in formulas for hydrologic calculations of design water discharge, flood level, and river flow velocity.

Adjustment factors to Rx1day for Viet Nam as a whole are based on changes (%) between a baseline period (1986–2005) and four future periods (2016–2035, 2036–2055, 2056–2075, and 2076–2099), according to Rx1day series obtained from 16 climate models with credible simulations of rainfall over Southeast Asia. Representative (greenhouse gas) concentration pathway RCP8.5 is recommended by the Ministry of Natural Resources and Environment of Viet Nam (MONRE 2016, 89) for "permanent projects and long term plans." For illustrative purposes, the Gumbel distribution was fitted to each series to estimate values for required return periods.

National-scale adjustments to Rx1day for Viet Nam ignore regional variations in extreme daily rainfall changes. However, there is low confidence in the ability of climate models to simulate climate processes that influence regional-scale rainfall variability (e.g., El Niño–Southern Oscillation, monsoons, and tropical cyclones), so high levels of spatial precision are unwarranted. Nonetheless, Rx1day is expected to increase, consistent with the growth in the number of the most powerful tropical cyclones making landfall in Viet Nam. Large temperature-dependent changes in *hourly* rainfall extremes could occur under so-called "super-Clausius–Clapeyron" scaling conditions.

Mean Sea-Level Rise and High-End Water Levels

Sea-level rise (SLR) presents a significant threat to populations, coastal infrastructure, and land use worldwide. According to sensitivity analyses done earlier, Viet Nam is the country that is most vulnerable to 1 meter (m) of SLR in terms of exposed population, potential losses in gross domestic product (GDP), and threats to urban areas and wetlands. Historical records at fixed tide gauges in Viet Nam show that mean sea level rose by ~2.5 millimeters per year (mm/y) between the 1960s and the 1990s, and has risen since then by ~3.3 mm/y, with a mean SLR of ~4 mm/y along the central coast.

Sea-level projections compiled for each coastal province in Viet Nam show mean SLR values under RCP4.5 and RCP8.5 for the northern coast (Hon Dau–Deo Ngang pass) and the central coast (Deo Ngang–Hai Van pass). In each case, the mean values are the sum of the following components of global sea-level change: thermal expansion of the ocean, mass balance, dynamic meltwater contribution from the Greenland and Antarctic ice sheets and from melting land glaciers, groundwater contribution, and glacial isostatic adjustment. Regional rates of SLR for Viet Nam account for changes in local gravity through global water mass redistribution. The results indicate minor regional variations in SLR for Viet Nam.

More extreme, yet credible, SLR scenarios may be required for long-lived or highly risk-averse projects such as power stations, ports, major flood defense assets, and other critical infrastructure in the coastal zone. High-end water levels >12 m could occur by 2100 if credible values for storm surges, waves, and high tides and changes in tidal regime are added to upper-bound mean SLR estimates. Simplifying assumptions were made about future surge–wave–tide interactions and changes in storm severity and coastal morphology because the likelihood of such multi-hazards has yet to be fully explored. However, even more extreme water levels can be envisaged under some scenarios with abrupt SLR and changes in extreme wind speeds. Finally, land subsidence may be an additional threat in many coastal urban areas.

Worked Examples

Two worked examples demonstrate the application of the allowances for climate change in Viet Nam. These are (i) the flooding of the Bao Ninh–Hai Ninh coastal road in Quang Binh province; and (ii) coastal erosion due to SLR at Thinh Long in Nam Dinh province.

Flooding of the Bao Ninh–Hai Ninh coastal road. Planned upgrades to the coastal road between Bao Ninh and Hai Ninh in Quang Binh province are at risk from (i) high-intensity rainfall with insufficient flood conveyance through culvert sections; and (ii) inundation or damage resulting from storm surge–tide–wave interaction with SLR. Under Viet Nam national standards, culverts draining the coastal road must incorporate a climate change adjustment factor with a design frequency of 25 years based on daily rainfall data.

The 25-year adjustment factor for Rx1day during the life of the asset (2016–2035) is 25%. This increases the design discharge by 8.27 cubic meters per second (m^3/s), the water level by 0.15 m, and streamflow velocity by 0.50 meter per second (m/s), compared with the baseline Rx1day, for an 8-m-wide rectangular, concrete culvert. The level of the road embankment would need to be raised accordingly to provide enough freeboard, and the culvert aprons and wings would have to be strengthened to accommodate the higher stream-flow velocity.

However, local storm surge and maximum wave heights during typhoons can already add up to ~4 m and ~8 m, respectively, to nearshore sea levels along the central coast. When springtide effects are included, high-water levels could exceed 13 m, even without SLR from global warming. Although SLR makes a relatively modest contribution to high-end water levels, it progressively reduces the return period of extreme events.

Some stretches of the road are only 4 m above mean sea level or within 100 m of the shoreline. In this case, focusing on incremental climate adjustments to design criteria for *individual* structures could obscure large *contextual* risks from inundation and erosion of low-lying sections of the coastal road. Ideally, less exposed road-routing options would be considered at the project concept stage.

Coastal erosion due to SLR at Thinh Long. Surveys from the 1930s and satellite imagery show particularly severe erosion of the coast in Hai Hau district in the northern region. The shoreline near Thinh Long town in Nam Dinh province retreated by 40–50 meters per year (m/y) in 2003–2005, and the beach was lowered by about 1.7 m in 2010–2011. These high rates of coastal erosion are expected to accelerate under future SLR.

The SLR scenarios from Table ES2 and a coastal erosion model indicate the possibility that unprotected sections of the coastline at Thinh Long could erode by more than 100 m by the end of the 21st century. Depending on the climate scenario chosen, this translates into long-term average erosion rates of 0.4–1.1 m/y—an order of magnitude lower than that observed but not including the impact of waves and storm surges during typhoons.

Accordingly, simulations of coastal erosion were performed with credible scenarios for storm-surge height (2.5 m and 5 m) and duration (12 hours and 24 hours), without and with SLR (0 m and 1 m). The results suggest that unprotected sections of the coastline at Thinh Long could erode by 5–20 m during a single typhoon, depending on storm-surge properties and the assumed SLR. A storm surge of 5 m, plus 1 m of SLR, increases the modeled amount of erosion by ~29%, compared with the no-SLR scenario.

Cautionary Remarks

This knowledge product describes the rationale, procedures, and climate change adjustment factors that are potentially applicable to various sectors and stages of the asset life cycle because they

(i)   draw on credible scientific evidence, yet are also pragmatic, proportionate in terms of the effort involved, and reflective of key uncertainties;

(ii) adopt national engineering design standards and procedures (exemplified here by road projects in Viet Nam);

(iii) require modest amounts of data (for creating scenarios of changes in extreme rainfall, regional SLR, and high-end water levels); and

(iv) apply fully transparent calculations for common design parameters such as channel discharge, flow depth and velocity, mean sea level, storm surge and wave height, and coastal erosion.

The scientific uncertainty attached to some of the above parameters is significant, especially for extreme events with long (>20-year) return periods. This uncertainty is due in part to low confidence in the ability of climate models to simulate natural variability and *changes* in extreme weather phenomena (e.g., tropical cyclones) at the scale of interest. Using future extreme rainfall or sea levels in impact models (e.g., for simulating flood and coastal erosion) heightens the uncertainty. Therefore, when selecting scenarios of adjustment factors for DED, a precautionary approach—avoiding the use of climate ensemble mean changes—is recommended.

Given ongoing developments in climate research and modeling, institutional mechanisms are needed for the periodic review and updating of the advice given for effective project design. Tables of adjustment factors should be kept under scrutiny to ensure that allowances for climate change are consistent with the latest scientific knowledge and observed trends. Care should also be taken with the words used. *Standards* are prescriptive, whereas *advice* or *guidance* may be discretionary. Likewise, *must*, *should*, and *could* convey different amounts of latitude in project design. It is recommended that climate change adjustment factors be reviewed every 5–10 years.

Conclusions

The worked examples provided in this knowledge product refer to the specific design requirements for roads and component structures in Viet Nam. They are intended to improve the resilience of the project to climate change over the useful life of an asset. Although the design stage is emphasized, the entire asset life cycle should be considered. In the course of adapting to incremental climate changes, it is important to be mindful of existing threats. As shown here, a culvert built under an upgraded coastal road may be designed to cope with a future 25-year fluvial flood from the land but could still fail if sited in an area where flooding or damage from the sea is the main climate threat. In such cases, the most significant climate vulnerability is specified not at the design stage but at the project concept stage. Tables of climate change adjustment factors are helpful in both situations.

Aside from long-term monitoring of design variables (such as extreme rainfall, sea level, and wave heights), the evidence base for developing future guidance could be strengthened in several areas. Key knowledge gaps for Viet Nam (as well as for most other Asian countries) pertain to the following:

(i)   Local rates of vertical land movements due to tectonic processes or groundwater subsidence (especially for cities on river deltas);

(ii)   Catchment-specific variations in flood response to expected changes in regional climate patterns and land cover;

(iii)   Effect of future changes in coastal sediment budgets, morphology, and bathymetry on local surge and wave propagation, extreme sea levels, and patterns and rates of erosion; and

(iv)   Expected changes in other design-relevant variables (e.g., wind gust, significant wave height and direction, extreme air and water temperatures, evaporation, and sub-daily rainfall intensities).

More generally, there may be scope for capacity development and training of project teams in the application of these climate change adjustments and procedures. Standard spreadsheets and look-up tables could be created to enable the rapid estimation of design parameters according to the national context and to sector- and project-specific information. Libraries of past extreme events, with accompanying data, could be compiled for stress-testing designs.

Finally, there is a limit to what can be achieved through generic guidance on allowing for site-specific climate threats in DED. Nonetheless, the underlying principles and procedures set out in this knowledge product offer a point of departure for more sophisticated assessments of high-risk projects.

1   Introduction

Climate change is expected to intensify heavy rainfall and raise global sea levels. More intense rainfall occurs because a warmer atmosphere holds more water—at least ~6.5% more per degree Celsius, according to the laws of thermodynamics (Allen and Ingram 2002). Higher sea levels result from thermal expansion of the ocean, combined with ice melt from land, local gravity effects, vertical land movements, and changes in ocean currents. Without adaptation and resilience measures, heavier rainfall and higher sea levels are likely to increase river and coastal flood risk.

The Midterm Review of Strategy 2020 (ADB 2014c) of the Asian Development Bank (ADB) set out a vision for mainstreaming adaptation and climate resilience in project planning, design, and implementation. As a result, all ADB infrastructure projects now undergo mandatory screening to identify those at high or medium risk of being adversely affected by climate change. At-risk projects must then be "climate-proofed" and made resilient to identified climate change impact.

The ADB climate risk management framework (CRMF) (ADB 2014a; ADB 2014b) helps project teams identify climate change risks to project performance at the start of the project cycle, and then to incorporate adaptation measures in the design of projects that are deemed to be at high or medium risk. The CRMF has 20 steps spread over three project phases. These phases are (i) concept (with climate-risk screening); (ii) preparation (with assessment of climate risk and vulnerability); and (iii) implementation (with monitoring and evaluation).

Economic analysis of adaptation options lies at the heart of the project preparation phase and rests on the identification, then the valuation, of engineered and nonengineering adaptation options (ADB 2015). Engineered adaptation options might include levees or coastal defenses; nonengineering options could consist of early-warning systems, land use zoning, or environmental solutions (see ADB 2014a). In all cases, there should be explicit benchmarking of the economic analysis of the project design with and without climate change, *as well as* with and without climate adaptation measures (to demonstrate incremental costs and benefits).

National engineering design standards are routinely based on intensity–duration–frequency (IDF) tables for hydrologic events. These tables provide extreme-value estimates for design variables such as extreme rainfall, sea level, storm surge height, wind speed, wave height, and air and water temperature. Such values were previously estimated from statistical distributions fitted to historical records, with a stationary time series as the key assumption. Although most historical *annual* rainfall records may be stationary (Sun, Roderick, and Farquhar 2018), under climate change this position could become untenable, so other methods for estimating design values had to be invoked (Milly et al. 2002). Now, adjustments to extreme-value distributions can be based on expected changes in the same quantities shown in climate models.

This knowledge product describes the rationale and procedures for incorporating allowances for climate change in the detailed engineering design (DED) of a project. Attention is focused on credible adjustments to rainfall and sea level, but the same approaches can be applied to other design variables (such as extreme air temperature, evaporation, and wind speed). Ultimately, the confidence vested in adjustments depends on the uncertainty in climate-model simulations of design variables at the project scale (see Pol and Hinkel 2019). From relatively high to low confidence, the variables are global mean air temperature and sea level (high); regional sea level, rainfall, and monsoon systems (medium); and local rainfall, wind, and wave heights (low) (Flato et al. 2013). Dealing with climate-model uncertainty is therefore an important aspect of the procedures.

This knowledge product is part of broader international efforts to issue practical guidance on incorporating climate change in design standards and the economic appraisal of adaptation measures (Box 1). It was drafted within the framework of the guidelines for the Basic Infrastructure for Inclusive Growth (BIIG) projects of the Viet Nam road transport sector and the specific institutional context of those projects. As part of this work, the ADB project preparatory technical assistance (PPTA) team developed climate change–adjusted rainfall projections for use within hydrologic formulas for estimating future peak flows and flood levels (ADB 2018).

Box 1: National Guidance on Climate Change Adjustments for Project Design

There are surprisingly few examples of climate change guidelines issued by national governments. Their terminology and rationale also vary. Some refer to *adjustments,* others to *allowances* or *risk reduction standards*. Some guides are intended to shape asset design; others, for sensitivity (or *stress*) testing of the performance of options. The legal status of the guidelines may cover a broad range extending from mandatory design standards through to advice that supports investment decisions. However, all emphasize the need for underpinning with robust scientific evidence, with due acknowledgment of technical uncertainties. Early guidance invoked the precautionary principle to improve flood resistance. For example, MAFF (2001) prescribed a blanket 20% change in peak river flows for testing projects in the United Kingdom for effectiveness under climate change over an assumed 50-year lifetime. Subsequent advice for the country provides upper, central, and lower allowances that vary with region and period (2020s, 2050s, and 2080s). Other analyses advocate climate change allowances based on catchment type (e.g., Broderick et al. 2019). However, as guidance becomes more elaborate, there is a greater risk of inconsistent interpretation and implementation. See the Further Reading section of this knowledge product for other examples of guidance on climate change adjustments to project design.

Source: Consultant's formulation.

The following procedures for road-design practice are intended for other sectors and stages of the asset life cycle (Table 1). Efforts to reduce climate risk to assets should begin at the concept stage, when managing exposure may be more effective than incorporating risk-reduction measures or retrofitting at the operating phase (Hallegatte 2009). For this reason, there will always be a place for hazard mapping and risk zoning. As will be shown later, identifying potential climate threats at the site selection (concept) stage could preempt the need for costly adaptations at the design stage. Climate risks at the construction stage include the impact of extreme weather on occupational health and the safety of workers, and disruption to supply chains. These risks are not discussed in this knowledge product.

Infrastructure operations may be affected by a host of climate risks. For instance, an intake to a water treatment plant sited near an estuary may be affected by future sea levels and storm surges leading to saltwater ingress. More stringent allowances for climate change may be required for the operational safety of assets, such as design floods for reservoir spillways (Veijalainen and Vehviläinen 2008). Some very long-lived utilities, like power plants in the coastal zone, must consider safe decommissioning, site remediation, and security for hazardous waste, perhaps in the context of sea-level rise over centuries (Wilby et al. 2011).

Table 1: Infrastructure Categories and Asset Life Stages

Infrastructure Category	Asset Life Stage				
	Concept	Design	Construction	Operation	Decommissioning
Aviation	o	x		o	
Bridges	o	x		o	
Dams	o	x		o	o
Drinking water	o	x		o	
Energy	o	x		o	o
Hazardous waste	o	x		o	o
Inland waterways	o	x		o	
Irrigation	o	x		o	
Levees	o	x		o	
Ports	o	x		o	
Railways	o	x		o	
Roads	o	x		o	
Schools	o	x		o	
Solid waste management	o	x		o	
Transit	o	x		o	
Wastewater	o	x		o	

o = applicability of aspects of the climate change adjustments to the concept, construction, operation, and decommissioning stages of an asset; x = applicability of adjustments for extreme rainfall and sea level for major infrastructure types.
Source: Adapted from LCE (2015) and ASCE (2017).

All asset categories listed in Table 1—whether an airport, bridge, mass transit system, port, power plant, or wastewater treatment facility—involve provisions for rainwater drainage or for fluvial and coastal flood defense systems. The procedures in this knowledge product for estimating extreme rainfall and sea-level rise are therefore widely applicable. However, some categories of infrastructure require adjustments to other climate variables such as extreme air temperatures (for estimating future crop water needs to size irrigation systems) and wind gusts (for bridge and airport design). Much rarer events than the 25-year return period considered here must be factored into design and operating procedures where there are safety standards (e.g., dam and bridge safety). These special cases require bespoke assessment and fall outside the scope of the present knowledge product.

2 Purpose and Scope

This knowledge product describes the rationale and procedures for incorporating climate change allowances in project design. The workflow generates climate change adjustments to extreme rainfall, channel discharge, and coastal erosion used in DED of roads and associated infrastructure. The various steps are demonstrated with worked examples drawn from the Viet Nam road transport sector (ADB 2018) and from peer-reviewed research literature. But the principles and practices adopted here are intended to be transferable to other sectors, regions, and stages of the asset life cycle.

The term *adjustment factor* is used throughout to mean the change in a design variable (e.g., 25-year return period, 1-day maximum rainfall) for a specified time horizon (e.g., 2030s), with respect to a defined baseline period (e.g., 1986–2005). Where feasible, some indication of the range of scientific uncertainty is given. All tables of adjustment factors presented here are based on Global Climate Model (GCM) output from the Coupled Model Intercomparison Project, Phase 5 (CMIP5) (Taylor, Stouffer, and Meehl 2012). Unless stated otherwise, a high-emission scenario—Representative Concentration Pathway RCP8.5—is assumed. (Other climate-model products, such as the National Aeronautics and Space Administration's Earth Exchange Global Daily Downscaled Projections (NEX-GDDP[1]), at 25-kilometer-resolution daily temperature and precipitation, are available but require file conversion.)

The scope of this knowledge product is restricted to adjustment factors for (i) 1-day annual maximum rainfall total (Rx1day); (ii) mean sea-level rise (SLR); and (iii) high-end water level. Tables of factors and consequences for design, using sites in central and northern Viet Nam, are presented. For an earlier set of extreme-rainfall and sea-level tables, see MONRE (2016). Other knowledge products may be issued later for variables such as sub-daily rainfall intensity, extreme air temperature, evaporation, and drought index.

Although climate hazards are treated separately here, it is important to recognize that they can be concurrent. For instance, within the Asia and Pacific region, tropical cyclones typically bring heavy rainfall, with high wind speeds, waves, and storm surges. Therefore, the DED should reflect the possibility of climate-driven changes in *multi*-hazards at a site.

The next section describes the steps in, and general features of, the adjustment procedure developed by the PPTA team for extreme rainfall, with entry points to mandatory formulas and design standards (ADB 2018). The section after that deals with mean sea and high-end water levels. Two worked examples show how tables of climate change adjustment factors are applied in practice. The final section identifies some key knowledge gaps and opportunities for further development of the guidance.

---

[1]   https://cds.nccs.nasa.gov/nex-gddp/.

Assumptions and Procedures for Extreme Rainfall Estimates

The following procedures are based on two premises. First, historical hydrometeorological records do not adequately represent the extreme climate conditions lying in store for long-lived structures. Second, climate models yield reliable information about *changes* in extreme-weather variables at the scale needed for engineering design.

The assumption of non-stationarity is widely accepted, and there is abundant observational evidence showing changes in rainfall and hydrologic extremes (IPCC 2012) with growing potential for human impact due to an increasingly urbanized global population (McPhillips et al. 2018). Various statistical techniques and analytical frameworks have been developed for estimating non-stationary return periods of climatic extremes (e.g., Cheng et al. 2014; Fowler and Kilsby 2003; Mertz et al. 2014). A widely adopted approach (used here) is to refit the parameters of an extreme value distribution to subperiods of the non-stationary climate series (e.g., Wilby and Wigley 2002). New extremes can then be calculated for the required return periods and future time horizon.

The assumption of GCM accuracy in representing future extreme rainfall at regional and daily scales is hard to defend (Flato et al. 2013). Numerous bias-correction and downscaling techniques have therefore emerged to bridge the gap between the coarse spatial scales of GCMs and the local scales needed for design variables (Fowler, Blenkinsop, and Tebaldi 2007). High-resolution dynamic models predict a global increase in the frequency of most intense tropical cyclones and associated heavy rainfall, but there remains considerable uncertainty about future changes for individual ocean basins (Knutson et al. 2010).

A realistic simulation of the present climate is a necessary but insufficient test of the accuracy of future climate changes shown by GCMs (Knutti et al. 2010) and downscaling (Racherla, Shindell, and Faluvegi 2012). For instance, the majority of GCMs in CMIP5 struggle to reproduce El Niño variability and persistence (Chen et al. 2017; Yun, Yeh, and Ha 2016). Across Southeast Asia, there are "significant biases" or "implausible" northeast and summer monsoons in the following GCMs: FGOALS-g2, inmcm4, IPSL-CM5B-LR, MIROC-ESM, MIROC-ESM-CHEM, MRI-CGCM3, and Nor-ESM1-M (McSweeney et al. 2015). Other models with errors in atmospheric circulation over the region are MIROC5, ACCESS1-3, and IPSL-CM5A-LR. All these models were excluded from subsequent rainfall analyses in this knowledge product.

Given the above limitations and uncertainties attached to climate-model projections, the question then arises as to how such information can be applied in smart ways. The recommended approach is to use only credible climate models (see above) to "bound" a range of plausible future changes (Clark et al. 2016; Smith et al. 2018). However, it is important to recognize that probabilities based on the distribution of output from climate-model ensembles are not equivalent to real-world probabilities. The choice of percentile from that distribution will also depend on how risk-averse the decision or design should be, as more precautionary solutions are likely to be more costly (Beven 2011). Here, the overall approach is risk-averse to reflect scientific and socioeconomic uncertainties, as well as the longevity of structures. For this reason, RCP8.5 was applied, with the threshold set at the 97.5th percentile of the climate-model ensemble range for extreme rainfall. As will be shown later, a precautionary approach was also followed for mean SLR and for high-end sea levels.

Figure 1 illustrates a procedure for adjusting extreme-rainfall estimates for DED. As shown, an initial set of adjustment factors was developed for each province in Viet Nam based on one regional climate model (PRECIS) driven by three GCMs (CNRM-CM5, GFDL-CM3, and HadGEM2-ES) under RCP8.5 (ADB 2018). This knowledge product follows the same procedure but draws on a larger CMIP5 ensemble (16 GCMs), also under RCP8.5 but without downscaling. Moreover, average adjustment factors are provided for the whole of Viet Nam rather than at the provincial level.

The above refinements are justified, since the primary source of uncertainty up to the mid-21st century arises from the choice of climate model, combined with natural variability (Hawkins and Sutton 2010; Deser et al. 2014). Although technically feasible, downscaling *all* CMIP5 simulations for Viet Nam would be prohibitively costly. Even then, some question whether downscaling improves the accuracy (as opposed to the precision) of regional climate change projections (Racherla, Shindell, and Faluvegi 2012). For instance, a 10-kilometer climate-model ensemble run by Australia's Commonwealth Scientific and Industrial Research Organisation (CSIRO) projected changes in mean Rx1day of –5% to +7% by 2045–2065, compared with model biases of 25% to 225% (Katzfey, McGregor, and Suppiah 2014).

Figure 1: Procedure for Incorporating Climate Change Allowances in Detailed Engineering Design

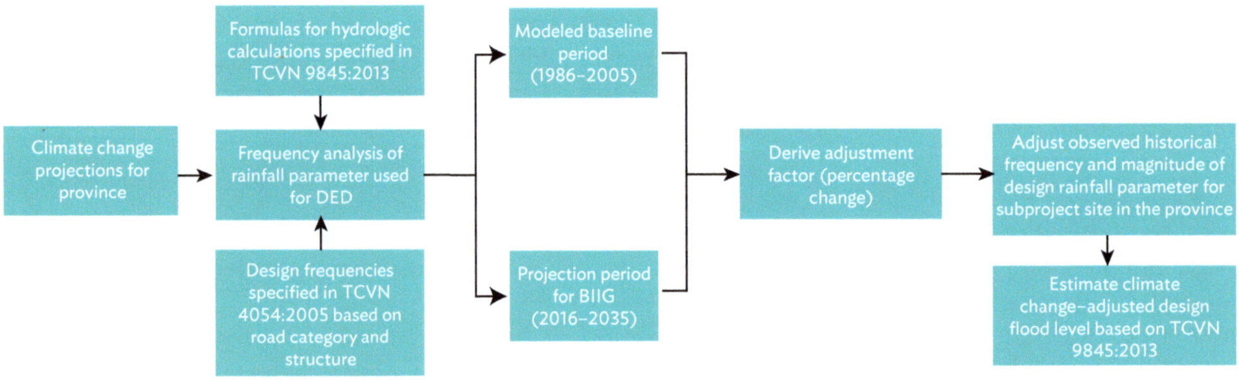

BIIG = Basic Infrastructure for Inclusive Growth (projects), DED = detailed engineering design, TCVN = Technical Committee of Vietnam.
Source: ADB (2018).

Specific climate variables (of given duration and return period) are typically mandated under national design standards for structures. For example, the Viet Nam national standards for roads (TCVN 4054:2005) and bridges (TCVN 9845:2013) require a design flood level of 1 in 100 years for expressways, and 1 in 25 years for category 3, 4, or 5 rural roads (Figure 1). In Viet Nam, the 1-day annual maximum rainfall total (Rx1day) is a critical variable in all formulas for hydrologic calculations of design water discharge, flood level, and flow velocity. Accordingly, this variable is given special attention.

The risk of structure failure depends on the standard of protection, the expected life of the asset, and the occurrence of extreme-weather events. According to the binomial distribution, the likelihood that an event will exceed design limits within a given period is surprisingly high (Table 2). For example, a culvert designed to accommodate a 25-year flood has a ~34% chance of exceedance within a 10-year period, and an ~87% chance in 50 years. If climate reduces the return period to 20 years and there are no adaptations to the design, the chance of exceedance in 10 and 50 years rises to ~40% and ~92%, respectively.

Table 2: Probability of at Least One Event Exceeding Design Limits during the Expected Life of a Structure

Return Period of Event (years)	Expected Life of Structure (years)			
	10	25	50	100
10	0.6513	0.9282	0.9948	1.0000
25	0.3352	0.6396	0.8701	0.9831
50	0.1829	0.3965	0.6358	0.8674
100	0.0956	0.2222	0.3950	0.6340

Source: Consultant's formulation.

Values of Rx1day were initially derived by the PPTA team from PRECIS experiments for a baseline (1986–2005) and two future periods (2016–2035, 2046–2065) (Figure 1). This knowledge product adopts the same baseline but provides fuller coverage of the 21st century by extracting Rx1day from credible models within the CMIP5 ensemble for (i) the baseline (1986–2005); (ii) the early 21st century (2016–2035); (iii) the early mid-21st century (2036–2055); (iv) the late mid-21st century (2056–2075); and (iv) the end of the century (2076–2095). The ensemble of 16 (rather than three) CMIP5 models makes it possible to sample a larger pool of climate change scenarios.

To demonstrate the procedure, the Gumbel distribution was fitted to the 20 annual maximum values drawn from each of the four future time periods to estimate Rx1day for five return periods (2, 5, 10, 20, and 25 years) and each climate model (Appendix 1). The estimation of longer return periods (e.g., 50 and 100 years) is defensible when larger samples of years are available—such as using 1956–2005 as a 50-year baseline. However, this increases the likelihood of non-stationarity within the longer series.

Derived adjustment factors are potentially sensitive to the choice of probability distribution (see Appendix 1). Gumbel was applied here for illustrative purposes because of its widespread acceptance, parsimony, and ease of parameter estimation (Menabde, Seed, and Pegram 1999). However, other distributions such as the three-parameter Generalized Extreme Value (GEV) distribution may be more locally appropriate (see ADB 2018).

All adjustment factors for Rx1day are given as percentage changes with respect to the baseline (Figure 1). These calculations can be susceptible to sample bias when a small ensemble of models is used. There is also the relatively large "noise" of natural climate variability compared with the climate change signal, especially for early decades (as illustrated in Figure 2 and Figure A1.3). Deploying a larger CMIP5 ensemble allows a wider range of initial model conditions (and, hence, natural climate variability) to be covered, yielding more robust sampling of climate-model projections of Rx1day (Hawkins and Sutton 2010).

Figure 2: Historical and Future Annual Rx1day for Viet Nam[a]

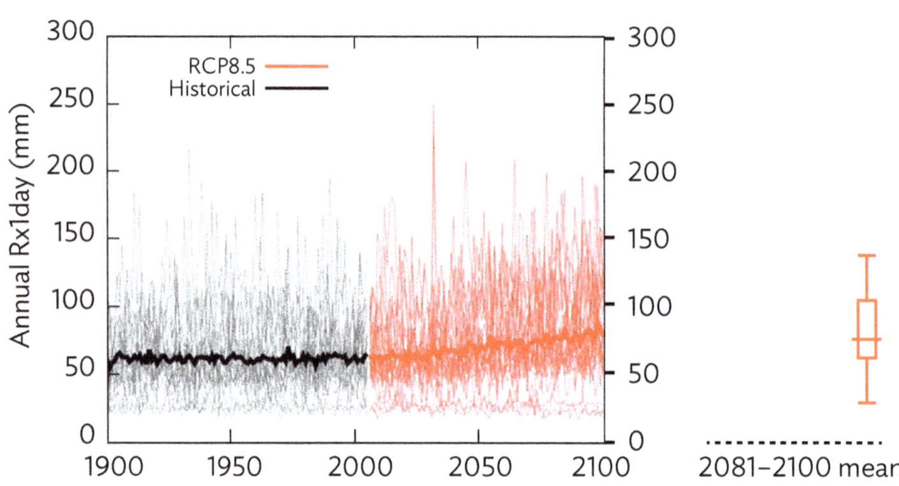

CMIP5 = Coupled Model Intercomparison Project, Phase 5; mm = millimeter; RCP = representative (greenhouse gas) concentration pathway; Rx1day = 1 day annual maximum rainfall total.

[a] Projected for the full CMIP5 Ensemble under RCP8.5. Note the interannual and inter-model variability shown by individual lines.

Source: KNMI Climate Explorer. http://climexp.knmi.nl/plot_atlas_form.py.

Climate change adjustment factors (% change) are used to scale site-specific baseline values of Rx1day (millimeters [mm]) at the required return period mandated for the asset category or structure type (Table 3). For example, small bridges and culverted crossings for rural roads in Viet Nam are designed to withstand the Rx1day with 25-year return period. From Table 3, the adjustment factor for the 25-year event by 2016–2035 is 25%. Given a baseline (1986–2005) Rx1day of 338 mm, the adjusted Rx1day for hydrologic calculations becomes 423 mm (see Appendix 2).

Table 3: Climate Change Adjustment Factors for Rx1day in Viet Nam
(%)

Future Period	Return Period (years)				
	2	5	10	20	25
2016–2035	15	20	25	25	25
2036–2055	35	25	30	30	35
2056–2075	50	45	45	45	45
2076–2095	80	75	75	70	70

Rx1day = 1-day annual maximum rainfall total.

Note: Based on Coupled Model Intercomparison Project, Phase 5 (CMIP5), under representative (greenhouse gas) concentration pathway RCP8.5. Return-period estimates are from the Gumbel distribution. All changes are relative to 1986–2005, for the 97.5th percentile of the credible ensemble, rounded up to the nearest 5%.

Source: Consultant's formulation.

National-scale adjustments of Rx1day for Viet Nam (Table 3) ignore possible regional variations in changes in extreme daily rainfall (Figure 3). However, as mentioned before, there is low confidence in the ability of climate models to simulate tropical cyclones and major modes of climate variability (such as El Niño); hence, higher levels of spatial precision are unwarranted. Furthermore, there is no seasonal breakdown, and all adjustment factors are rounded up to the nearest 5% to avoid a false impression of precision. Overall, Rx1day is expected to increase, consistent with the growth in the number of the most powerful tropical cyclones making landfall in Viet Nam since 1990 (MONRE 2016).

**Figure 3: Projected Changes (%) in Extreme Daily Rainfall
in the Various Regions of Viet Nam**

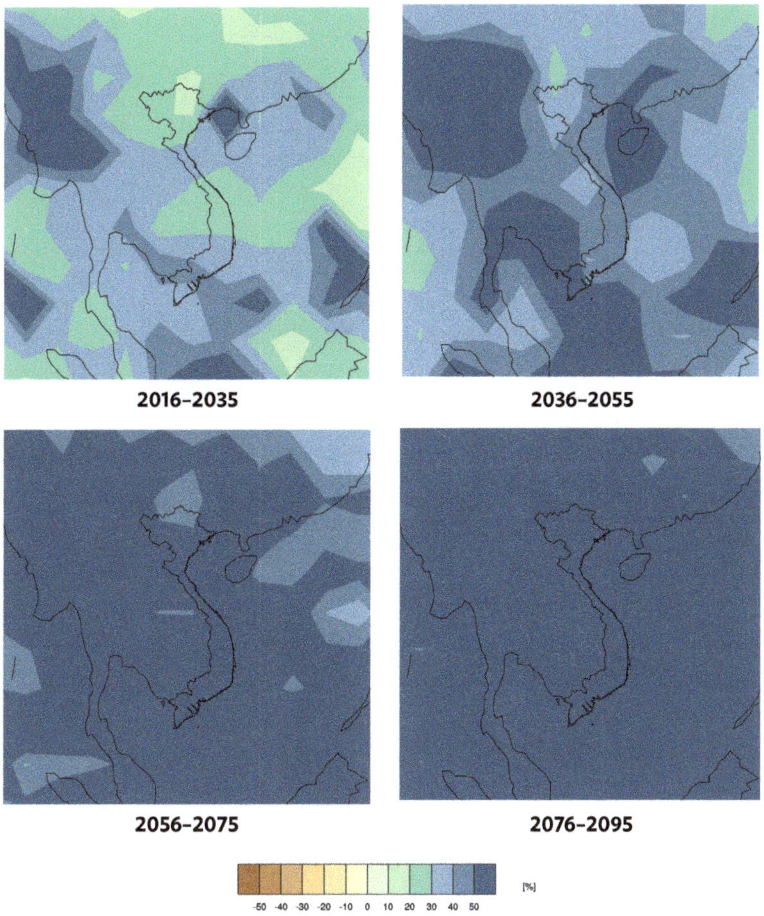

Note: All changes are relative to 1986–2005, for the 97.5th percentile of Rx1day in the full CMI5 ensemble.
Source: KNMI Climate Explorer. http://climexp.knmi.nl/plot_atlas_form.py.

Note that the adjustment factors presented in Table 3 apply to changes in daily rainfall extremes, which are expected to follow Clausius–Clapeyron scaling (~6.5%/°C). However, pluviograph records across Australia suggest that temperature-related increases in hourly rainfall extremes can be close to or even exceed twice the Clausius–Clapeyron scaling (Guerreiro et al. 2018). Super-Clausius–Clapeyron scaling of hourly rainfall is possible when there is large-scale upward motion and moisture convergence in the atmosphere, driven by near-surface increases in dewpoint temperature (Lenderink et al. 2017). Future temperature-scaling of hourly rainfall extremes will depend on regional variations in the weather patterns favoring convective precipitation (Schroeer and Kirchengast 2018), as well as on the source areas of moisture, cloud size, and extent of organized convection (Lochbihler et al. 2017).

Sea-level rise is a significant threat to populations, coastal infrastructure, and land use worldwide (Hallegatte et al. 2013). According to World Bank sensitivity analyses, Viet Nam is the country that is most vulnerable to 1 meter (m) of SLR in terms of exposed population, potential losses in gross domestic product (GDP), and threats to urban areas and wetlands (Dasgupta et al. 2009a). Moreover, a 10% increase in storm-surge height combined with a 1 m SLR could expand the area of the storm-surge zone in Viet Nam by 35% (Dasgupta et al. 2009b).

Records of mean sea level in Viet Nam from fixed tide gauges confirm that water height is rising at most sites (Figure 4). Observed SLR rates over the last 20 years average +2.2 millimeters per year (mm/y) in the north (Hon Dau), +4.1 mm/y in the center (Da Nang), and +0.9 mm/y in the south (Vung Tau).

Figure 4: Annual Mean Sea Level Recorded at Tide Gauges in Viet Nam

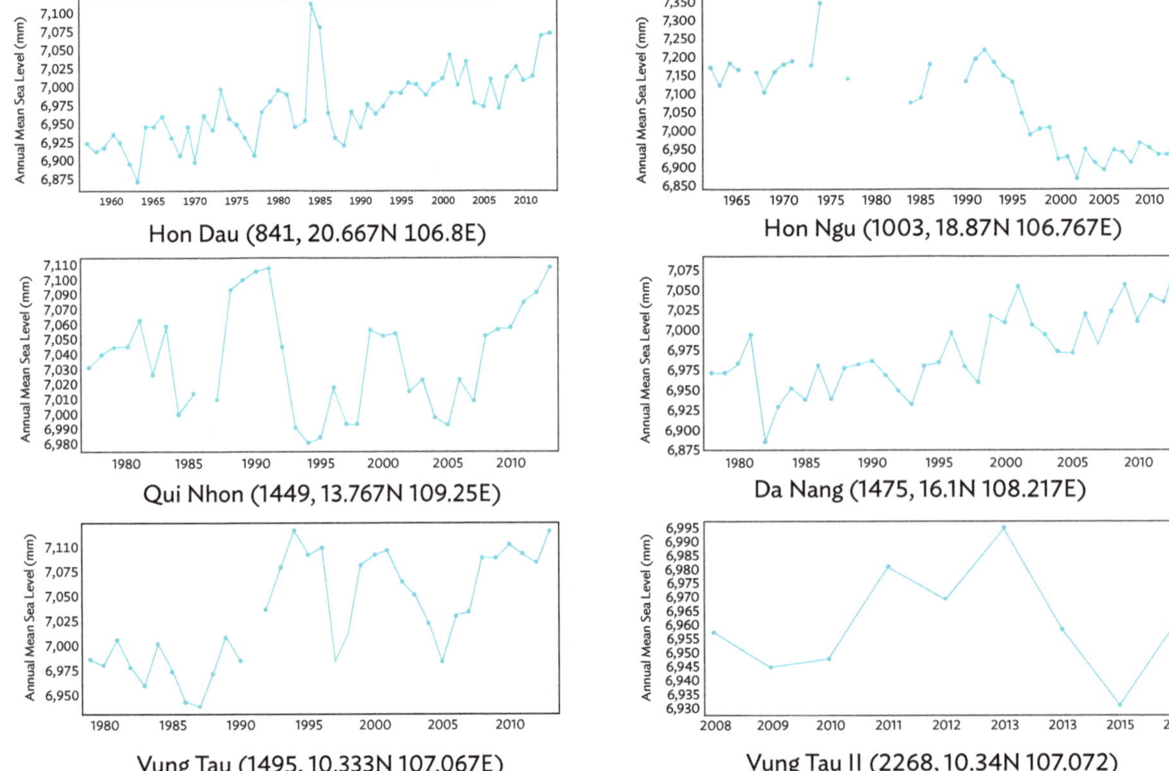

mm = millimeter.
Note: Numbers within parentheses are station codes, latitude, and longitude.
Source: Permanent Service for Mean Sea Level.

However, the interpretation of some trends is confounded by the brevity of records (in the case of Vung Tau II) or by known station moves (Hon Ngu). Overall, sea level rose by ~2.5 mm/y between the 1960s and the 1990s, and has risen by ~3.3 mm/y since then, with a mean SLR of ~4 mm/y along the central coast (MONRE 2016).

Sea-level projections were compiled by MONRE (2016) for each coastal province in Viet Nam. Tables 4 and 5 show the expected rise under RCP4.5 and RCP8.5 for the northern coast (Hon Dau–Deo Ngang pass) and the central coast (Deo Ngang–Deo Hai Van pass). In each case, mean values (and uncertainty ranges within parentheses) are based on the CMIP5 ensemble (Church et al. 2013). Values are the sum of the following components of global sea-level change: thermal expansion of the ocean, mass balance, dynamic meltwater contribution from the Greenland and Antarctic ice sheets and from melting land glaciers, groundwater contribution, and glacial isostatic adjustment. Regional rates of SLR for Viet Nam reflect an adjustment for changes in local gravity through global water mass redistribution (Slangen et al. 2014). Note that the scenarios shown in Tables 4 and 5 do not include the effects of storm surge, tides, waves, tectonic uplift, or subsidence. The differences in the mean SLR scenarios between the northern and central regions are minor.

Table 4: Mean SLR Scenarios for Hon Dau–Deo Ngang (Northern Coast)
(cm)

Scenario	2030	2040	2050	2060	2070	2080	2090	2100
RCP4.5	13 (8–18)	17 (10–24)	22 (13–31)	27 (16–39)	33 (20–47)	39 (24–56)	46 (28–65)	53 (32–75)
RCP8.5	13 (9–18)	18 (12–26)	25 (17–35)	32 (22–45)	40 (28–57)	50 (34–71)	60 (41–85)	72 (49–101)

cm = centimeter, RCP = representative (greenhouse gas) concentration pathway, SLR = sea-level rise.
Note: Under RCP4.5 and RCP8.5. All changes are relative to 1986–2005. Values within parentheses are uncertainty ranges.
Sources: Tables 6.5 and 6.7 in MONRE (2016).

Table 5: Mean SLR Scenarios for Deo Ngang–Deo Hai Van (Central Coast)
(cm)

Scenario	2030	2040	2050	2060	2070	2080	2090	2100
RCP4.5	13 (8–18)	17 (11–24)	22 (13–32)	28 (17–39)	34 (20–47)	40 (24–56)	46 (28–65)	53 (32–75)
RCP8.5	13 (9–18)	19 (13–26)	25 (17–35)	33 (22–46)	41 (28–58)	50 (34–71)	61 (41–86)	72 (49–102)

cm = centimeter, RCP = representative (greenhouse gas) concentration pathway, SLR = sea-level rise.
Note: Under RCP4.5 and RCP8.5. All changes are relative to 1986–2005. Values within parentheses are uncertainty ranges.
Sources: Tables 6.5 and 6.7 in MONRE (2016).

The mean SLR scenarios shown in Figure 5 are useful in several different ways. They can be

(i)   added to observed mean sea level to identify vulnerable sites or to evaluate sensitivity to coastal impact within geospatial analysis (as in Dasgupta et al. 2009a; Dasgupta et al. 2009b), and thus inform land-use zoning, project screening, or site selection at the concept stage;

(ii)   applied in DED or for stress-testing different design options (as in Wilby et al. 2011), to identify potential "cliff edge" effects, whereby even a modest increase in SLR can produce abrupt changes in coastal flooding or erosion risk (with or without adaptation measures); and

(iii)   used within a robust decision-making framework (Lempert et al. 2006), emphasizing "satisficing" rather than optimization, and combining options and decision criteria in ways that minimize regret for a wide range of plausible scenarios or imprecise probability distributions.

Figure 5: SLR Scenarios for Deo Ngang–Deo Hai Van

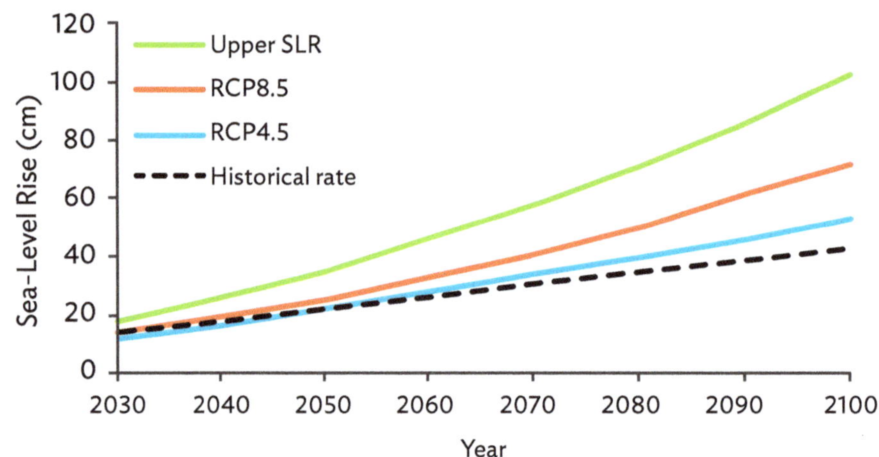

cm = centimeter, RCP = representative (greenhouse gas) concentration pathway, SLR = sea-level rise.
Note: The upper SLR curve is based on the upper-bound values in Table 5 for RCP8.5. The historical rate is extrapolated from observations at Da Nang.
Source: Consultant's formulation.

More extreme, yet credible, SLR scenarios may be required for long-lived or highly risk-averse projects such as power stations, ports, major flood defense assets, and other critical infrastructure in the coastal zone (as in Ranger, Reeder, and Lowe 2013). Credible maximum SLR scenarios have already been used to develop flood-protection strategies at whole-city (e.g., New York; see Rosenzweig et al. 2011) and even nationwide scales (e.g., the Netherlands; see Katsman et al. 2011). A case can also be made for exploring extreme global-warming scenarios (Nicholls et al. 2011) or projections that extend beyond the 21st century (Solomon et al. 2009), given institutional path dependencies, lock-in of coastal infrastructure, and the likely irreversibility of SLR for centuries to come (Smajgl et al. 2015).

As with mean SLR, a component-based approach (Nicholls et al. 2014) was followed in constructing high-end water-level scenarios for Viet Nam. Potential drivers of rapidly (R) and slowly (S) changing high water levels include the following:

(i)   Storm surges (R) due to low pressure associated with the passage of a tropical cyclone (Neumann et al. 2015; Thuy et al. 2017);

(ii)   Significant wave height and direction (R) (Dastgheib et al. 2016; Nagai, Kono, and Quang 1998; Osinowo et al. 2016);

(iii)   Interacting wind, wave, tide, and surge effects (R) (Thai et al. 2017);

(iv)   Interannual variations in mean and extreme sea level due to the El Niño–Southern Oscillation (S) (Muis et al. 2018);

(v)   Changes in tidal regime (S) (Thuc and Son 2012);

(vi)   Vertical land movements (S) due to sedimentation, erosion, and tectonic uplift (Schimanski and Stattegger 2005); and

(vii)   Subsidence (S) linked to groundwater exploitation or compaction of delta sediments (Erban, Gorelick, and Zebker 2014; Minderhoud et al. 2017).

High-end water levels >12 m by 2100 (Tables 6 and 7) are achieved when credible values for components are added to upper-bound mean SLR estimates (Tables 4 and 5). However, the following simplifying assumptions are made: (i) maximum surge and wave heights will remain the same as at present; (ii) extreme surges, waves, and tides will behave independently of one another; (iii) vertical land movements due to tectonic processes and changes in coastal sediment budgets can be neglected; and (iv) coastal morphology or bathymetry will remain the same as at present. Land subsidence can be an additional threat in many coastal urban areas (e.g., Yin, Yu, and Wilby 2015). The net effects of these assumptions may be conservative high-end scenarios. On the other hand, some studies suggest more extreme tropical cyclones (Wang, Liang, and Hodges 2017) and an upper-bound mean SLR estimate of 2 m by 2100 (Nicholls et al. 2011), so high water levels could be more extreme.

Likelihoods cannot be assigned to high-end water-level components, and their respective uncertainties are assumed to be mutually independent. Monte Carlo methods can be used to estimate upper and lower bounds if uncertainties in components are specified as mutually dependent (Meehl et al. 2007). As a result, there is uncertainty in individual water-level components as well as different ways of combining component means and their various uncertainty ranges (such as by quadrature or linearly, independently or dependently). This means that transparency of evidence for components and calculations is essential.

Table 6: High-End Water-Level Components for Hon Dau–Deo Ngang (Northern Coast) (cm)

Scenario	2030	2040	2050	2060	2070	2080	2090	2100
Upper SLR	18	26	35	45	57	71	85	101
Surge	490	490	490	490	490	490	490	490
Wave	425	425	425	425	425	425	425	425
High tide	185	185	185	185	185	185	185	185
Tidal regime	4	5	7	9	11	14	17	20
Total	1,122	1,131	1,142	1,154	1,168	1,185	1,202	1,221

cm = centimeter, SLR = sea-level rise.

Notes: Under representative (greenhouse gas) concentration pathway RCP8.5. All changes are relative to 1986–2005. *Upper SLR* is the upper bound of the uncertainty range for RCP8.5. *Surge* is the highest storm that might occur in Quang Ninh–Thanh Hoa. *Wave* is the maximum recorded wave during typhoons at Hai Hau station. *High tide* is the maximum amplitude for Ba Lat. *Tidal regime* adds 20% of *mean SLR* to reflect changes in long wave resonance in deeper water.

Sources: Tables 6.7 and 6.8 in MONRE (2016); Pruszak et al. (2002); Thuc and Son (2012).

Table 7: High-End Water-Level Components for Deo Ngang–Deo Hai Van (Central Coast)
(cm)

Scenario	2030	2040	2050	2060	2070	2080	2090	2100
Upper SLR	18	26	35	46	58	71	86	102
Surge	420	420	420	420	420	420	420	420
Wave	800	800	800	800	800	800	800	800
High tide	90	90	90	90	90	90	90	90
Tidal regime	4	5	7	9	11	14	17	20
Total	1,332	1,341	1,352	1,365	1,379	1,395	1,413	1,432

cm = centimeter, SLR = sea-level rise.

Notes: Under representative (greenhouse gas) concentration pathway RCP8.5. All changes are relative to 1986–2005. *Upper SLR* is the upper bound of the uncertainty range for RCP8.5. *Surge* is the highest storm that might occur in Quang Binh–Thua Thien Hue. *Wave* is the maximum wave height recorded at Da Nang during Typhoon Kaemi. *High tide* is the maximum amplitude for Da Nang. *Tidal regime* adds 20% of *mean SLR* to reflect changes in long wave resonance in deeper water.

Sources: Tables 6.8 and 6.9 in MONRE (2016); Tran et al. (2004).

Flooding of the Bao Ninh to Hai Ninh Coastal Road

The unpaved coastal road between Bao Ninh and Hai Ninh, Quang Binh province, is to be improved to promote tourism (ADB 2018). Upgrading to a category 5 plain road will involve widening the road, adding layers of base and sub-base, and surfacing the present road with asphalt concrete. Once completed, the 10.6 km road will have a surface elevation of 4–10 m above mean sea level. A new 600 m section will be built to bypass a commune at the southern end of the alignment. Two spillway–culvert crossings will be replaced, and 28 new culverts are proposed in addition to the existing 15 culverts.

Section of the Bao Ninh–Hai Ninh Coastal Road, Quang Binh Province. The planned improvement of the coastal road will include replacement of existing and construction of additional spillway-culvert crossings. (photo by ADB).

The planned structures are at risk from (i) high-intensity rainfall with insufficient flood conveyance through culverted sections; and (ii) flooding or damage by storm surge–tide–wave interactions with SLR. Viet Nam national standards TCVN 9845:2013 specify hydrologic calculations for road embankment heights, road drainage, and clearance of bridges above the design flood level (ADB 2018, 7). These require that culverts draining the coastal road incorporate a climate change adjustment factor with a design frequency of 25 years based on daily data. Other techniques are required to estimate changes in sub-daily rainfall extremes for urban drainage design (Box 2).

Box 2: Adjusting Extreme Sub-daily Rainfall Estimates

Intensity–duration–frequency (IDF) tables are widely used for designing hydraulic structures. Traditional approaches to the design of storm-water management systems assumed the stationarity of sub-daily rainfall extremes, but these are no longer credible, given observed and expected changes in intense rainfall. Various techniques for modifying IDF tables are being developed. These include the disaggregation of weather-generator output, the use of Bayesian frameworks fitted to the parameters of non-stationary extreme value distributions, the extrapolation of parameters from daily data, and the fractal scaling of intensities over different storm durations. Most of these techniques assume the availability of some sub-daily data for model calibration. See the Further Reading section for information about various methods of adjusting sub-daily extreme-weather statistics for climate change.

Source: Consultant's formulation.

The climate change adjustment procedure in Figure 1 was followed in calculating the 25-year design discharge (Q_{25}), water level (H_{25}), and streamflow velocity (V_{25}) for an upgraded spillway–culvert (see Appendix 2 for full technical details). The 25-year adjustment factor for Rx1day during the period 2016–2035 is 25% (Table 3). This increases Q_{25} by 8.27 cubic meters per second (m^3/s), H_{25} by 0.15 m, and V_{25} by 0.50 meters per second (m/s) compared with the historical rainfall, assuming an 8-m-wide rectangular, concrete cross section (Table 8). The level of the road embankment would need to be raised accordingly to provide enough freeboard, whereas culvert aprons and wings would have to be strengthened to accommodate the higher streamflow velocity.

Table 8: Design Discharge (Q_{25}), Water Level (H_{25}), and Stream-Flow Velocity (V_{25}) for a Spillway–Culvert on the Bao Ninh–Hai Ninh Coastal Road, Quang Binh Province

Design Basis	Q25 (m³/s)	H25 (m)	V25 (m/s)
25-year design frequency based on historical Rx1day	22.56	0.71	3.96
25-year design frequency based on RCP8.5 scenario Rx1day	30.83	0.86	4.46

m = meter, m³/s = cubic meter per second, m/s = meter per second, RCP = representative (greenhouse gas) concentration pathway, Rx1day = 1-day annual maximum rainfall total.
Note: Water levels are for the depth of stream flow in the structure *not* relative to a datum.
Source: Consultant's formulation.

Extreme rainfall and fluvial flooding are not the only climate-related threats to the coastal road. Viet Nam's coast is often hit by tropical cyclones, and evidence shows that more of these storm systems have made landfall in recent decades (Figure 7). Local surge and wave heights during typhoons can add up to ~4 m and ~8 m, respectively, to nearshore high water levels along the central coast (Table 7). When spring-tide effects are included, high water levels could exceed 13 m, even without SLR from global warming. Although tide–surge interactions are thought to be negligible, model experiments suggest that wave interactions can contribute up to 25% of the total surge level (Thuy et al. 2017), so tide–wave–surge interactions are not simply additive. High-resolution regional climate modeling also shows that there could be a shift in future tropical cyclone activity, with storms becoming more frequent in winter and less so in summer (Wang, Liang, and Hodges 2017).

Figure 6: Annual Frequency of Tropical Cyclones Making Landfall in Viet Nam

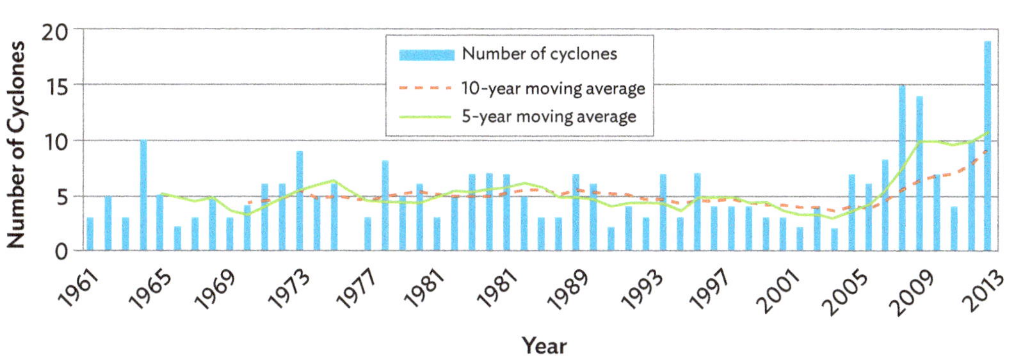

Source: Duc et al. (2017), based on data provided by the Viet Nam National Center for Hydro-meteorological Forecasting. Reprinted by permission from Springer Nature.

Sea-level rise makes a relatively modest contribution to high-end water levels but could progressively reduce the return period of extreme events (Neumann et al. 2015). Even conservative estimates of combined tide–wave–surge heights suggest that low-lying sections of the Bao Ninh–Hai Ninh road are already at risk from flooding and storm damage during tropical cyclones. Some stretches of the road are only 4 m above mean sea level or within 100 m of the shoreline. Viet Nam design standards provide for the possibility that historical maximum floodwater levels could be higher than the flood levels derived from frequency analysis (ADB 2018). Under such circumstances, the historical floodwater level is to be used. However, it is unclear what design adjustments should be made if maximum flood levels are due to inundation by the sea rather than from land.

Sections of the Bao Ninh–Hai Ninh Coastal Road, Quang Binh Province. Flooding and storm damage during tropical cyclones may affect low-lying sections of the coastal road. (Map data: Google, CNES / Airbus, DigitalGlobe).

In Viet Nam, overtopping of category 5 road elevations is permitted at crossings of wide and shallow riverbeds or at sites with localized depressions and slow-flowing water. Allowable maximum depths for submersible crossings depend on streamflow velocity and type of vehicle, ranging from 0.2 m for nonmotorized vehicles passing through water flows of more than 2 m/s, up to 0.7 m for motorcycles and small tractors crossing streams with the same flow rate. Under storm-surge conditions, these allowances could conceivably be exceeded on some sections of the coastal road.

Parts of the road may also be vulnerable to coastal erosion. Quang Binh province has 50 km of eroded coast (Thao, Takagi, and Esteban 2014), with some sections eroding by 40–60 m per year (Tien et al. 2005). More specifically, Bao Ninh was identified as an erosion hot spot at the 11th meeting of the Asia-Pacific Economic Cooperation (APEC) Emergency Preparedness Working Group in 2017.

By focusing on climate adjustments to design criteria for *individual* structures, project planners may overlook *wider* risks of inundation and erosion of low-lying sections of the coastal road. As shown in Table 1, climate risks could be addressed at other stages in the asset life cycle. Ideally, at the concept stage, less exposed options for road routing might be considered. During project design, more storm-resistant or storm-resilient materials and structures could be used. A range of structural solutions could be deployed to protect the coast (Duc et al. 2017), but these may not be appropriate, given the high amenity value of the coastal dune systems and the need for access to the beach. In this case, nonengineering options such as dune protection, beach nourishment, or the planting of mangrove forests may be preferred (see Box 3 below). During operation, budgets and schedules for road maintenance may have to be revised, depending on storm frequency and the level of (recurrent) damage.

Coastal Erosion Due to Sea-Level Rise at Thinh Long

Viet Nam's 3,260-km-long coastline is highly vulnerable to SLR, coastal flooding, and erosion (Hanh and Furukawa 2007). Wind fields from climate models fed into numerical wave and sediment transport models suggest substantial variations in potential longshore transport for the northern, central, and southern parts of Viet Nam. An increase in net transport rates of up to 0.5 million cubic meters per year (m^3/y) is predicted at some locations even without SLR (Dastgheib et al. 2016).

Topographic maps dating from the 1930s and satellite imagery show particularly severe coastal erosion in Hai Hau district in the northern region (Figure 9). Erosion rates in 1965–1985 averaged 21 meters per year (m/y) at Hai Ly, 5 m/y at Hai Dong, and 11 m/y on the Hai Chinh–Hai Thinh coast (Duc et al. 2017). More recently, the most rapid erosion has been occurring on the coast of Thinh Long town in Nam Dinh province, where the shoreline retreated by 40–50 m/y in 2003–2005, and the beach was lowered by about 1.7 m in 2010–2011.

Figure 7: Photographic Evidence of Rapid Erosion along the Hai Hau Coast

(a) Hai Trieu commune in 1995 (L.G. Vu, 2003)

(b) Hai Trieu commune in 1995 (L.G. Vu, 2003)

(d) Hai Ly commune in September 2011

(e) Hai Ly commune in July 2010

Source: Source: Duc et al. (2017). Reprinted by permission from Springer Nature.

Scenarios of coastal erosion were created from historical and projected rates of SLR for Hon Dau to Deo Ngang (shown in Table 4), combined with beach and wave parameters for Thinh Long (Duc et al. 2017). For illustrative purposes, this information was fed into the coastal erosion model of Brunn (1962) to simulate the cumulative retreat of the shoreline over the period 2030–2100. This model is applicable to shorelines with sand dunes and assumes that (i) the profile shape of the retreating beach is unaffected by geology; (ii) there is no offshore transport (beyond *closure depth*) or longshore transport of eroded sediments; (iii) there is no effect from offshore features such as sandbars; and (iv) particle grain size is the only determinant of the equilibrium beach profile (Pilkey et al. 1993). Overall, the main challenge when calibrating the model is in defining the maximum sea depths at which sediment exchange occurs between beaches and offshore zones as a result of wave disturbance (Healy 1996). Technical details of the model are summarized in Appendix 3.

Simulations with the Brunn (1962) model suggest that unprotected sections of the coastline at Thinh Long could erode by more than 100 m by the end of the 21st century (Figure 10). This translates into long-term average erosion rates of 0.4–1.1 m/y, depending on the climate-model scenario, compared with 0.2 m/y due to historical SLR. The projected rates of erosion are of an order of magnitude lower than observed (see the second paragraph of this subsection) but do not include the impact of waves and storm surges during tropical cyclones.

Figure 8: Sea-Level Rise Scenarios for Hon Dau–Deo Ngang (left panel) and Cumulative Coastal Erosion Scenarios for Thinh Long (right panel)

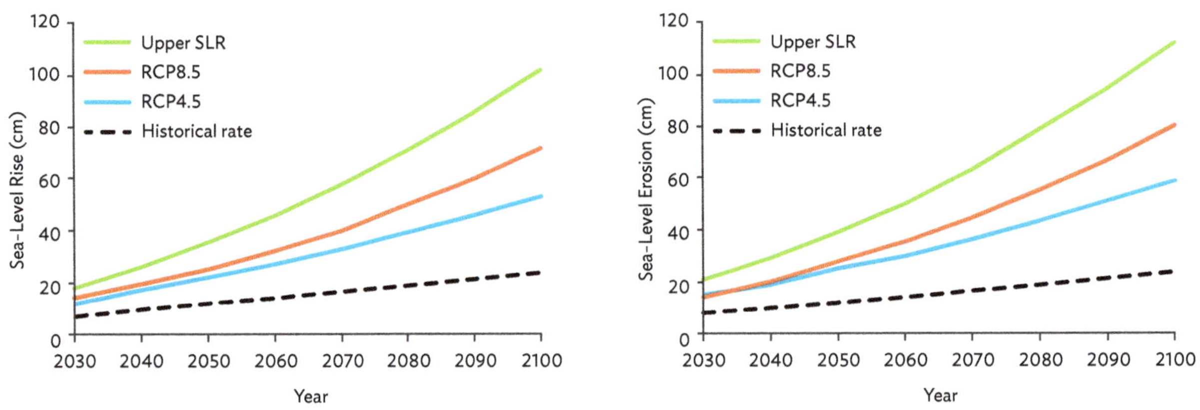

cm = centimeter, RCP = representative (greenhouse gas) concentration pathway, SLR = sea-level rise.
Note: The historical rate of sea-level rise is extrapolated from observations at Hon Dau.
Source: Consultant's formulation.

Scenarios of coastal erosion during storm surges are illustrated using the model of Kriebel and Dean (1993), with beach and wave parameters for Thinh Long (Duc et al. 2017). Rather than simulating the shoreline response to gradual changes in sea level over decades, this model applies unsteady-state conditions, with higher storm-water levels lasting up to several days. As before, simplifying assumptions about uniform changes in beach profile, offshore and longshore sediment transport processes, and the equilibrium profile apply. In addition, the model makes the unrealistic assumption that upper parts of the beach profile (the berm) erode throughout the duration of the storm, rather than only at the time of peak water level (Kriebel and Dean 1993).

Six simulations of coastal erosion were performed with the Kriebel and Dean (1993) model, using credible scenarios for storm-surge height (2.5 m and 5 m) and duration (12 hours and 24 hours), without and with SLR (0 m and 1 m). Model results suggest that unprotected sections of the coastline at Thinh Long could erode by 5–20 m during a single typhoon, depending on storm-surge properties and assumed SLR (Figure 11). A storm surge of 5 m plus 1 m of SLR increases the modeled amount of erosion by ~29% compared with the no-SLR scenario.

Figure 9: Coastal Erosion Scenarios at Thinh Long for Storm Surges of Varying Height and Duration, and with Sea-Level Rise (lower panels)

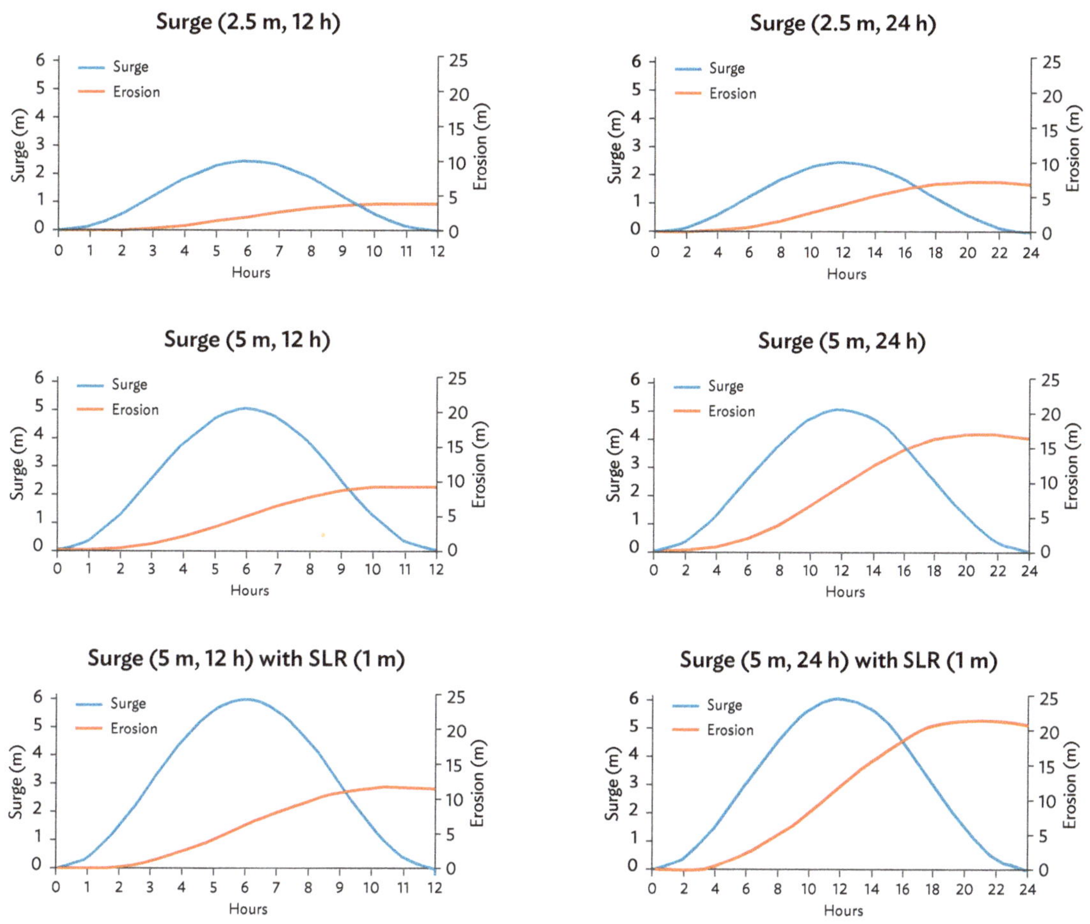

h = hour, m = meter, SLR = sea-level rise.
Note: See Appendix 3 for model details.
Source: Consultant's formulation.

Storm surges plus SLR increase the risk of wave overtopping, and erosion of the crest and inner slope of coastal dikes, leading to the possibility of structural failure. Erosion rates will vary according to the geometric and geotechnical properties of the materials used in the dike. Rates as high as 50 centimeters per hour (cm/h) can occur where the inner slope is bare soil and there is no vertical wall to prevent wave run-up (Duc et al. 2017). Under RCP8.5, erosion rates for dikes with bare soils could be 10 times higher than at present.

There are several structural and nonstructural measures for improving coastal protection, depending on the predicted severity of local erosion (Figure 12). Research in Viet Nam has been at the forefront of adaptation policy and practice development (Box 3). Engineering solutions might consist of reinforcing soil dikes with concrete groins; (re)planting mangrove forests to promote sediment accretion and protection where erosion rates are <2 m/y; raising dike heights and deepening footings; locating standby blocks nearby for emergency repairs during storm conditions; incorporating natural geo-textiles and planting vetiver grass on inner slopes that suffer from overtopping; or building offshore, submerged breakwaters (such as geo-tubes) to dissipate wave energy (Duc et al. 2017).

Figure 10: Coastal Protection Options for Adapting to Climate Change with Different Severities of Erosion

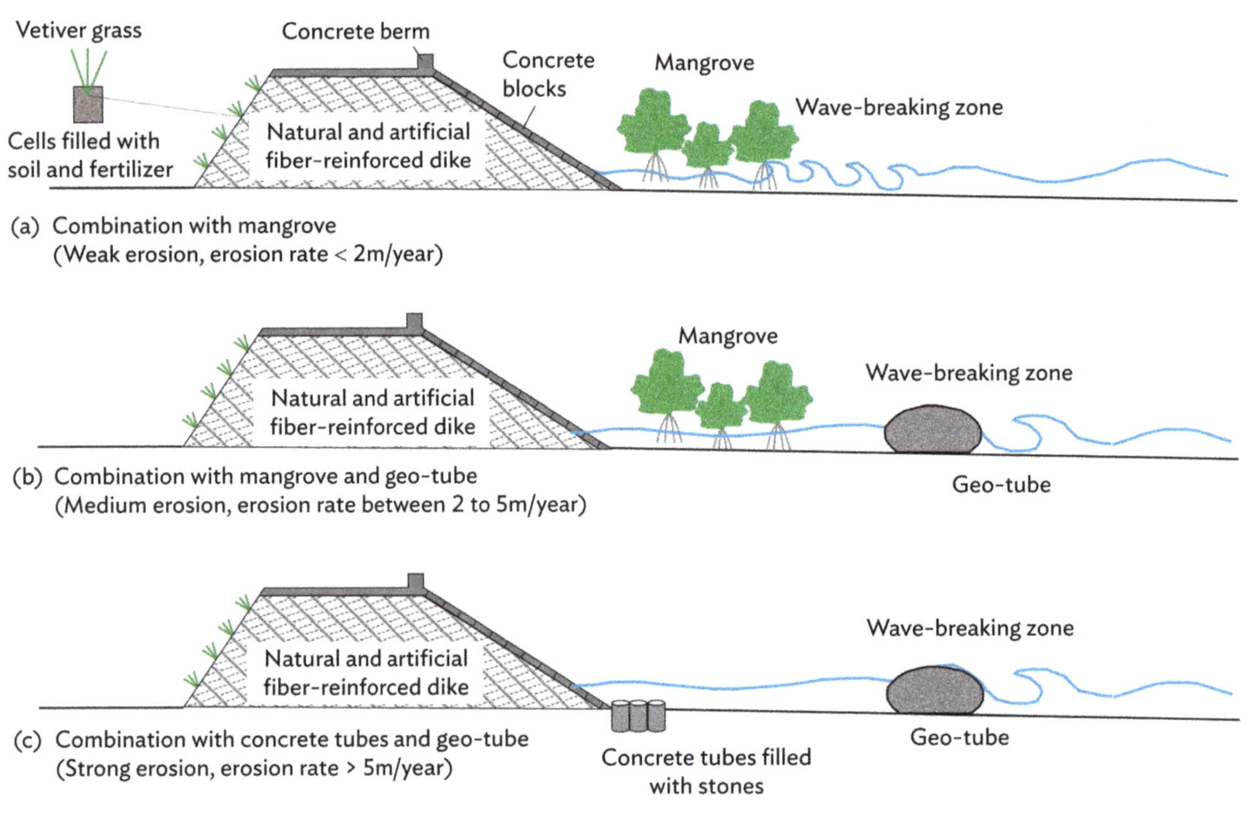

m = meter.
Source: Source: Duc et al. (2017). Reprinted by permission from Springer Nature.

Box 3: Adaptation Policy and Practice in the Coastal Zone

Some seminal research into climate change adaptation has been undertaken in Viet Nam. Early work in the northern coastal region showed how vulnerability to climate change is socially and geographically differentiated. Poverty indicators revealed those households that were most likely to be exposed to climate hazards yet least able to gain access to resources following a catastrophe. Therefore, equitable adaptation processes and measures must be devised to address these realities. A good test is to ask who benefits most from the proposed adaptation measures, and who might be disadvantaged (for instance, by reduced adaptive capacity or loss of livelihood). Other studies have developed very specific adaptation guidance. For example, empirical equations, based on field data collected in Viet Nam, show the minimum band width and mangrove forest structure needed to attenuate a maximum wave height of 3 meters down to a 30-centimeter wave. See the Further Reading section for more information about adaptation case studies and syntheses of approaches.

Source: Consultant's formulation.

6   Concluding Remarks

This knowledge product describes the rationale, procedures, and climate change adjustment factors that are potentially applicable to various sectors and stages of the asset life cycle because they

(i)   draw on credible scientific evidence, yet are also pragmatic, proportionate in terms of the effort involved, and reflective of key uncertainties;

(ii)   adopt national engineering design standards and procedures (exemplified here by road projects in Viet Nam);

(iii)   require modest amounts of data (for creating scenarios of changes in extreme rainfall, regional SLR; and high-end water levels); and

(iv)   apply fully transparent calculations for common design parameters such as channel discharge, flow depth and velocity, mean sea level, storm surge and wave height, and coastal erosion.

The scientific uncertainty attached to some of the above parameters is significant, especially for extreme events with long (>20-year) return periods. This uncertainty is due in part to low confidence in the ability of climate models to simulate natural variability and *changes* in extreme weather phenomena (e.g., tropical cyclones) at the scale of interest. Using future extreme rainfall or sea levels in impact models (e.g., for simulating flood and coastal erosion) heightens the uncertainty. Therefore, when deriving adjustment factors for DED, a precautionary approach is recommended.

Given ongoing developments in climate research and modeling, institutional mechanisms are needed for the periodic review and updating of the advice given for project design. Tables of adjustment factors should be kept under scrutiny to ensure that allowances for climate change are consistent with the latest scientific knowledge and observed trends. Care should also be taken with the words used. *Standards* are prescriptive, whereas *advice* or *guidance* may be discretionary. Likewise, *must, should,* and *could* convey different amounts of latitude in project design. It is recommended that climate change adjustment factors be reviewed every 5–10 years.

The illustrative rainfall and sea-level adjustments described in this knowledge product refer to the specific design requirements for roads and component structures in Viet Nam. They are intended to improve the resistance of the project to climate change over the useful life of an asset. Although the design stage is emphasized, the entire asset life cycle should be considered. In the course of adapting to incremental climate changes, it is important to be mindful of existing threats. As shown here, a culvert built beneath an upgraded coastal road may be designed to cope with a future 25-year fluvial flood but could still fail if sited in an area where flooding or damage from the sea is the main climate threat. In such cases, the most significant climate vulnerability is identified not at the design stage but at the project concept stage. Tables of climate change adjustment factors are helpful in both situations.

Aside from long-term monitoring of design variables (such as extreme rainfall, sea level, and wave heights), the evidence base for developing future guidance could be strengthened in several areas. Key knowledge gaps for Viet Nam (as well as for most other Asian countries) pertain to the following:

(i) Local rates of vertical land movements due to tectonic processes or groundwater subsidence (especially for cities on river deltas);

(ii) Catchment-specific variations in flood response to expected changes in regional climate patterns and land cover;

(iii) Effect of future changes in coastal sediment budgets, morphology, and bathymetry on local surge and wave propagation, extreme sea levels, and patterns and rates of erosion; and

(iv) Expected changes in other design-relevant variables (e.g., wind gust, significant wave height and direction, extreme air and water temperatures, evaporation, and sub-daily rainfall intensities).

More generally, there may be scope for capacity development and training of project teams in the application of these climate change adjustments and procedures. Standard spreadsheets and look-up tables could be created to enable the rapid estimation of design parameters according to national context and to sector- and project-specific information. Libraries of past extreme events, with accompanying data, could be compiled for stress-testing designs.

Finally, there is a limit to what can be achieved through generic guidance on allowing for site-specific climate threats in DED. Nonetheless, the underlying principles and procedures set out in this knowledge product offer a point of departure for more sophisticated assessments of high-risk projects.

Extreme-Rainfall Estimation

Gumbel Distribution

The estimation of baseline and future extreme rainfall amounts rests on the assumption that the annual maxima are approximately distributed as a Generalized Extreme Value (GEV) distribution. There are three types of GEV distribution: (i) the Gumbel distribution (type I) is unbounded and useful when data are normally or exponentially distributed; (ii) the Fréchet distribution (type II) is bounded at the lower tail; and (iii) the Weibull distribution (type III) is bounded at the upper tail (Figure A1.1).

Figure A1.1: Comparison of the Probability Density Functions of the Three Types of Generalized Extreme Value Distribution

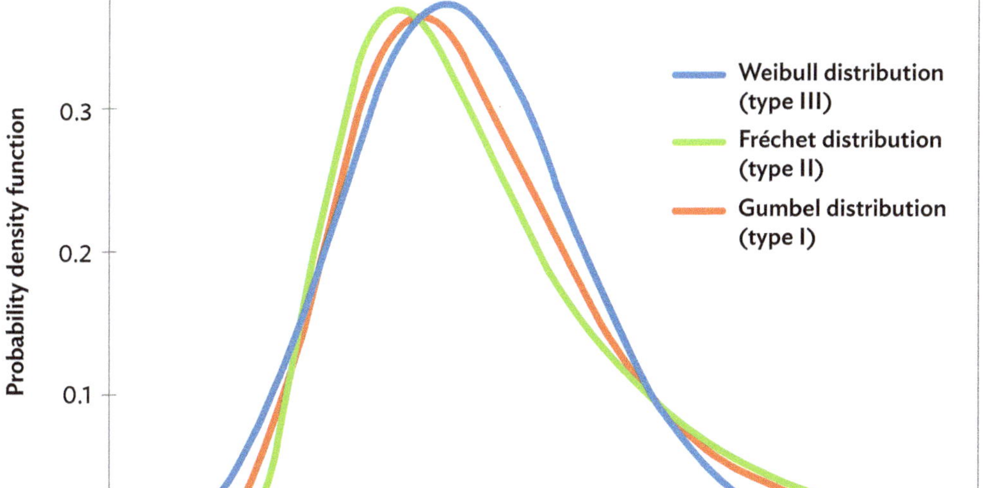

GEV = Generalized Extreme Value.
Source: https://www2.cisl.ucar.edu/sites/default/files/penult16.pdf.

The Gumbel type was applied here because the distribution is unbounded and has only two parameters, which are readily calculated through the method of moments (Wilks 1995):

$$\sigma = \frac{s\sqrt{6}}{\pi} \tag{A1.1}$$

$$\mu = \bar{x} - \gamma\sigma \tag{A1.2}$$

where σ is the scale parameter, s is the sample standard deviation, μ is the location parameter, $\bar{x}$ is the sample mean, and γ is the Euler constant (0.577). Note that for the Gumbel distribution, the GEV shape parameter equals zero.

Quantiles q_T of the Gumbel distribution are given by the following formula:

$$q_T = \mu - \sigma \ln\left(-\ln\left[1 - \tfrac{1}{T}\right]\right) \tag{A1.3}$$

where T is the return period (years).

The standard error s_e of Gumbel estimates of q_T may also be derived through the method of moments (Kite 1988, Su and Tung 2013) using this formula:

$$s_e^2 = \frac{\sigma^2}{n}(1.15894 + 0.19187Y + 1.1Y^2) \tag{A1.4}$$

$$Y = -\ln\left(-\ln\left[1 - \tfrac{1}{T}\right]\right) \tag{A1.5}$$

where n is the sample size and the 95% upper/lower confidence limit q_L is given by this formula:

$$q_L = q_T \pm 1.96 s_e \tag{A1.6}$$

Table of R1xday Adjustment Factors

The climate change adjustment factors (%) for Rx1day in Table 3 were derived via the following six steps:

(i) Calculate the sample mean ($\bar{x}$) and standard deviation (s) of each credible CMIP5 ensemble member from the baseline annual Rx1day series;

(ii) Use Eq. A1.1 and Eq. A1.2 to estimate the Gumbel scale and shape parameter, respectively, for each annual series in step 1;

(iii) Use Eq. A1.3 to estimate Rx1day for T = 2, 5, 10, … 100 years (Figure A1.2a);

(iv) Repeat steps 1 to 3 using future annual Rx1day series (Figure A1.2b);

(v) Calculate the change (%) in Rx1day between the future and baseline for each ensemble member and return period (Figure A1.2c); and

(vi) Extract the upper bound (97.5th percentile) of the ensemble distribution of changes (Figure A1.2d) and round up to the nearest 5%.

Figure A1.2: Gumbel Estimates of Rx1day for Credible CMIP5 GCMs under (a) Baseline (1986–2005) and (b) Future (2076–2095) Climate Conditions,* with (c) Percentage Changes and (d) 95% Confidence Intervals

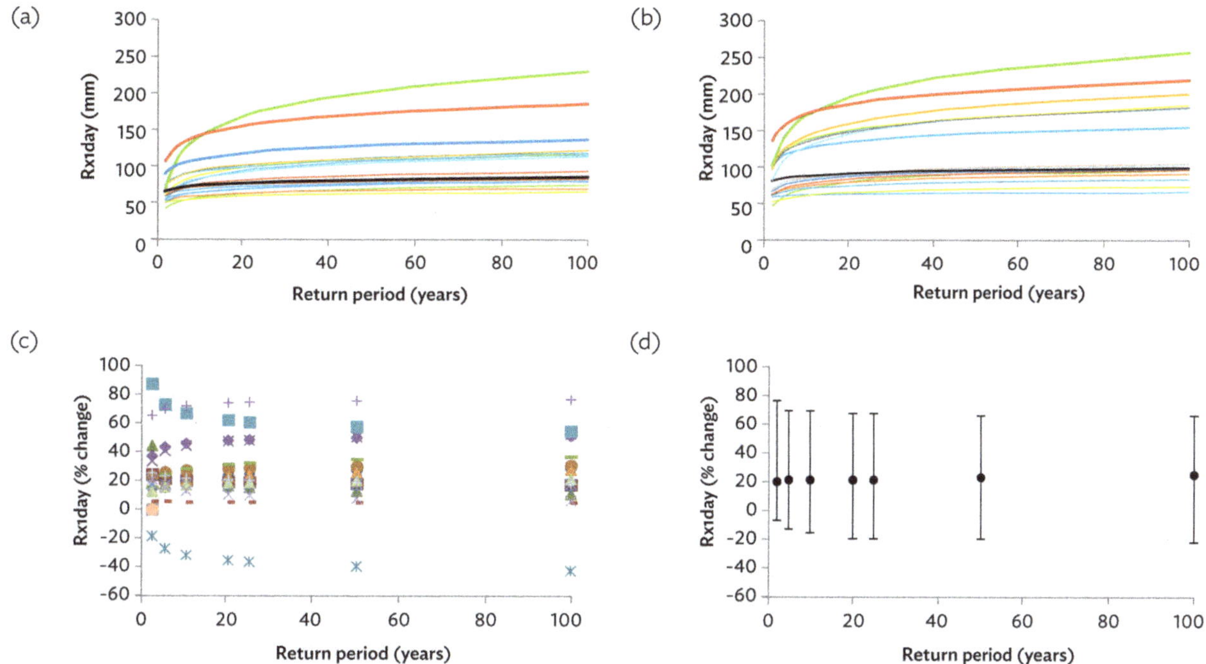

CMIP5 = Coupled Model Intercomparison Project, Phase 5; GCM = global climate model; mm = millimeter; Rx1day = 1-day annual maximum rainfall total.

* Colored lines show individual GCMs; the black line is the ensemble mean.

Source: Consultant's formulation.

Uncertainty Bounds for Rx1day Estimates

Uncertainty in the Rx1day estimates varies according to climate model, return period, time horizon, emission scenario, and choice of extreme value distribution. For example, the sampling error in the Gumbel Rx1day estimates can be derived by using Eq. A1.6 for each credible climate model and then added to the central estimate to give an upper-bound estimate for different return periods (Figure A1.3). This shows that in 2016–2035, projected changes in Rx1day compared with 1986–2005 are within the range of uncertainty of the Gumbel estimate for most climate models. By 2076–2095, the climate change signal is much stronger, such that projected changes in Rx1day are mostly greater than the 95% confidence range of the baseline estimate.

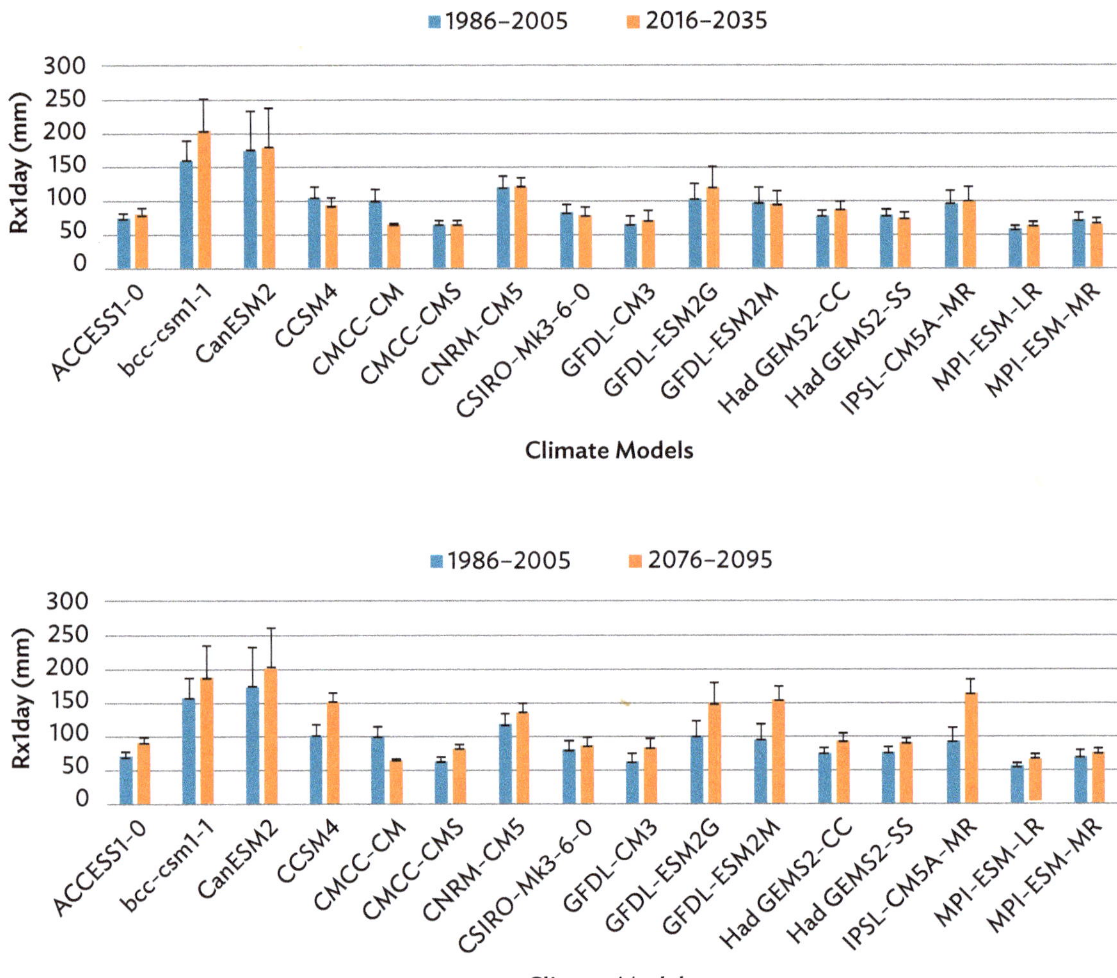

mm = millimeter, Rx1day = 1-day annual maximum rainfall total.

  * 95% confidence range, shown by T-bars.

** Based on output from credible climate models in 1986–2005 (baseline) compared with 2016–2035 (upper panel) and 2076–2095 (lower panel) under RCP8.5.

Source: Consultant's formulation

The Viet Nam extreme value analysis was based on a 20-year baseline as well as 20-year time slices for future periods, so change factors are limited to the 25-year return period in Table 3.

APPENDIX 2
Design Floods for Roads and Associated Structures

Scenarios of design water discharge (Q_p), water level (H_p), and water velocity (V_p) for return period p were developed for the case study site following the procedures set out in TCVN 9845:2013 for catchment areas of less than 100 square kilometers (km^2):

$$Q_p = A_p \varphi R_p F \delta \tag{A2.1}$$

where A_p is the flood peak module at design frequency p (taken from Table 6 of TCVN 9845:2013), φ is the flood flow coefficient (which depends on soil sand content θ, catchment area, and rainfall zone z, from Table A1 of TCVN 9845:2013), R_p is the 1-day annual maximum rainfall amount (mm) at design frequency p (for the baseline period 1986–2005), F is the catchment area (km), and δ is a flood reduction factor (determined by the extent of upstream surface water ponding by swamps and wetlands, from Table 6 of TCVN 9845:2013).

The next step is to create rating curves at the site or structure for the water level (H) and water velocity (V) as a function of discharge (Q), using the Chézy–Manning equations:

$$V = C(rm)^{1/2} \tag{A2.2}$$

$$C = \frac{1}{n} r^{1/6} \tag{A2.3}$$

$$r = \frac{\alpha}{\gamma} \tag{A2.4}$$

$$Q = \alpha V \tag{A2.5}$$

$$\omega = Hw \tag{A2.6}$$

where C is the Chézy coefficient ($m^{1/2}/s$), r is the hydraulic radius (m), m is the slope of the channel or culvert bed (m/m), n is Manning's roughness coefficient, α is the cross-sectional area of the water in the structure (m^2), γ is the wetted perimeter (length of water in contact with the structure) (m), and w is the width of the cross section (m). With Eq. A2.2 to Eq. A2.6 and a plausible range of Q, it is possible to develop rating curves for H and V (Figure A2).

Figure A2: Rating Curves for Water Depth (H) and Velocity (V) at the Study Site

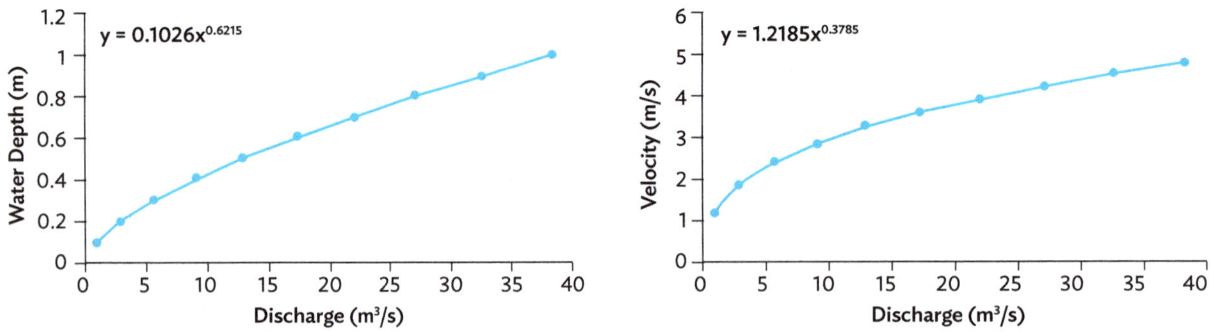

m = meter, m/s = meter per second, m³/s = cubic meter per second.

Source: Consultant's formulation.

Design values for H_p and V_p are calculated for the baseline period given the rating equations in Figure A2 and Q_p from Eq. A2.1. Design values reflecting future climate change are derived for Q_{pf} using this formula:

$$Q_{pf} = A_p \varphi R_p F \delta c^{1.4} \tag{A2.7}$$

where c is the climate change adjustment factor at the required design frequency p from Table 3. The exponent for c is 1.4 because the parameter A_p in Eq. A2.7 (and hence Q_p) indirectly depends on R_p, as follows:

$$A_p \sim R_p^{0.4} \tag{A2.8}$$

As before, Q_{pf} is applied to the rating equations to obtain adjusted design values for H_{pf} and V_{pf} at design frequency p. Table A2 gives example values for all 12 parameters needed to apply the above procedures to the case study site.

Table A2: Parameters Used to Calculate Design Discharge, Water Depth, and Flow Velocity through a Culvert beneath the Bao Ninh–Hai Ninh Coastal Road

Parameter	Description	Value (units)
p	Mandatory design frequency for small culverts	25 years
A_p	Flood-peak module	0.05
ϕ	Flood-flow coefficient	0.1
z	Rainfall zone	X
θ	Soil sand content	90%
R_p	1-day annual maximum rainfall with frequency p	338 mm
F	Catchment area	17.8 km²
δ	Flood-reduction factor	0.75
m	Slope of the culvert	0.01 m/m
n	Manning coefficient for concrete culvert	0.018
w	Width of the culvert	8 m
c	Climate change adjustment to R_p	25%

km² = square kilometer, m = meter, m/m = meter per meter, mm = millimeter.

Source: Consultant's formulation.

Sea-Level Rise, Storm Surge, and Coastal Erosion Models

Sea-Level Rise and Coastal Erosion

Scenarios of coastal erosion (R) were produced using the model of Brunn (1962) with beach-profile parameters for Thinh Long, Hai Hau district (Duc et al. 2017):

$$R = SLR \frac{L_*}{h_* + B}$$

(A3.1)

where SLR is the amount of sea-level rise (m), L_* is the width of the active beach profile (m), h_* is the depth of closure (m), and B is the height of the berm (m).

The model assumes that material eroded by SLR from the upper shore is deposited on the nearshore ocean bed. This leads to a shoreward displacement of the beach profile. The height of deposited material in the nearshore zone equals the rise in sea level, thereby maintaining a constant water depth.

Eq. A3.1, the parameters in Table A3.1, and sea-level rise scenarios in Table 4 give the following values for predicted cumulative coastal erosion at Thinh Long: 14–20 m by 2030, 24–39 m by 2050, and 59–112 m by 2100 relative to 1995. The respective amounts of erosion extrapolated from historic rates of SLR at Hon Dau (2.2 mm/y) are 9, 13, and 26 m.

Table A3.1: Parameters Used to Model Coastal Erosion Due to Sea-Level Rise Alone at Thinh Long

Parameter	Description	Value (units)
SLR	Historic rate of sea-level rise	2.2 mm/y
L_*	Width of the active beach profile	1,377.6 m
h_*	Depth of closure	10.4 m
B	Height of the berm	2 m

m = meter, mm/y = millimeters per year.
Source: Duc et al. (2017).

Storm Surge and Coastal Erosion

Storm-surge and coastal-erosion scenarios were produced using a convolution method for a time-dependent beach-profile response (Kriebel and Dean 1993) with beach and wave parameters for Thinh Long, Hai Hau district (Duc et al. 2017):

$$\frac{R(t)}{R_\infty} = \frac{1}{2}\left\{1 - \frac{\beta^2}{1+\beta^2}\,exp\left(-\frac{2\sigma t}{\beta}\right) - \frac{1}{1+\beta^2}[\cos(2\sigma t) + \beta\sin(2\sigma t)]\right\} \tag{A3.2}$$

where $R(t)$ is the amount of erosion (m) at a specified height in the beach profile t (hours) after storm onset, R_∞ is the maximum amount of erosion (m) after the system reaches equilibrium, β is the ratio of the erosion time scale (T_S) to the surge duration (T_D) from the start to the end of the water rise, given by this formula:

$$\beta = 2\pi\frac{T_S}{T_D} \tag{A3.3}$$

$$\sigma = \frac{\pi}{T_D} \tag{A3.4}$$

$$R_\infty = \frac{S(x_b - h_b/m)}{B + h_b - S/2} \tag{A3.5}$$

where S is the surge height (m), x_b is the width of the surf zone (m), h_b is the depth of water at the point of breaking waves (m), m is the beach slope (m/m), B is the height of the berm (m), and

$$x_b = \left(\frac{h_b}{A}\right)^{3/2} \tag{A3.6}$$

$$A = \left(\frac{\omega^2}{g}\right)^{1/3} \tag{A3.7}$$

where A ($m^{1/3}$) is a parameter that governs the shape of the beach profile depending on the coarseness of beach material, represented by the sediment fall velocity ω (cms^{-1}), and g is the acceleration due to gravity ($9.81\ ms^{-2}$).

The erosion timescale (T_S) in Eq. A3.3 is obtained from the following empirical expression:

$$T_S = 320\frac{H_b^{3/2}}{g^{1/2}A^3}\left(1 + \frac{h_b}{B} + \frac{mx_b}{h_b}\right)^{-1} \tag{A3.8}$$

where H_b is the height of breaking waves (m), which, unless specified, is assumed to equal $0.78h_b$. Finally, T_S in Eq. A3.8 is divided by 3,600 to convert the computed value to hours.

Sea-level rise is incorporated by raising the maximum storm-surge height by the specified amount(s). All other beach and wave properties are unchanged, and no adjustment is made for tidal variations. The beach, wave, and storm parameters used to model costal erosion at Thinh Long (Figure 10) are given in Table A3.2.

Table A3.2: Beach Profile and Wave Parameters Used to Model Coastal Erosion at Thinh Long

Parameter	Description	Value (units)
m	Linear slope of beach profile	0.01 m/m
h_b	Depth of water at the point of breaking waves	8.18 m
H_b	Height of breaking waves	3.78 m
B	Height of the berm	2 m
A	Beach material-profile parameter	0.084 $m^{1/3}$
S	Storm surge maximum height	2.5 m, 5 m
T_D	Storm surge duration	12 h, 24 h
g	Acceleration due to gravity	9.81 m/s^2

m = meter, $m^{1/3}$ = cube root of meter, m/m = meter per meter, m/s^2 = meter per second squared.
Source: Duc et al. (2017).

References

Allen, M. R., and W. J. Ingram. 2002. Constraints on Future Changes in Climate and the Hydrologic Cycle. *Nature*. 419. pp. 228–232.

American Society of Civil Engineers (ASCE). 2017. *Infrastructure Report Card*. https://www .infrastructurereportcard.org/ (accessed 27 August 2018).

Asian Development Bank (ADB). 2014a. *Climate Proofing ADB Investment in the Transport Sector: Initial Experience*. Manila.

————. 2014b. *Climate Risk Management in ADB Projects*. Manila.

————. 2014c. *Midterm Review of Strategy 2020: Meeting the Challenges of a Transforming Asia and Pacific*. Policy paper. Manila.

————. 2015. *Economic Analysis of Climate-Proofing Investment Projects*. Manila.

————. 2018. *Adjusting Hydrological Inputs to Road Design for Climate Change Risk Based on Extreme Value Analysis*. Report ADB PPTA 8957-VIE. Manila.

Beven, K. 2011. I Believe in Climate Change but How Precautionary Do We Need to Be in Planning for the Future? *Hydrological Processes*. 25 (9). pp. 1517–1520.

Brunn, P. 1962. Sea-Level Rise as a Cause of Shore Erosion. *Journal of the Waterways and Harbors Division*. 88 (1). pp. 117–132.

Chen, C., M. A. Cane, A. T. Wittenberg, and D. Chen. 2017. ENSO in the CMIP5 Simulations: Life Cycles, Diversity, and Responses to Climate Change. *Journal of Climate*. 30 (2). pp. 775–801.

Cheng, L., A. AghaKouchak, E. Gilleland, and R. W. Katz. 2014. Non-stationary Extreme Value Analysis in a Changing Climate. *Climatic Change*. 127. pp. 353–369.

Church, J. A., P. U. Clark, A. Cazenave, J. M. Gregory, S. Jevrejeva, A. Levermann, M. A. Merrifield, G. A. Milne, R. S. Nerem, P. D. Nunn, A. J. Payne, W. T. Pfeffer, D. Stammer, and A. S. Unnikrishnan. 2013. Sea Level Change. In: Stocker, T. F., D. Qin, G.-K. Plattner, M. Tignor, S. K. Allen, J. Boschung, A. Nauels, Y. Xia, V. Bex, and P. M. Midgley, eds. Climate Change 2013: The Physical Science Basis. Contribution of Working Group I to the Fifth *Assessment Report of the Intergovernmental Panel on Climate Change*. Cambridge University Press.

Clark, M. P., R. L. Wilby, E. D. Gutmann, J. A. Vano, S. Gangopadhyay, A. W. Wood, H. J. Fowler, C. Prudhomme, J. R. Arnold, and L. D. Brekke. 2016. Characterizing Uncertainty of the Hydrologic Impacts of Climate Change. *Current Climate Change Reports.* 2 (2). pp. 55–64.

Dasgupta, S., B. Laplante, C. Meisner, D. Wheeler, and J. Yan. 2009a. The Impact of Sea Level Rise on Developing Countries: A Comparative Analysis. *Climatic Change.* 93 (3–4). pp. 379–388.

Dasgupta, S., B. Laplante, S. Murray, and D. Wheeler. 2009b. Sea-Level Rise and Storm Surges: A Comparative Analysis of Impacts in Developing Countries. *Policy Research Working Paper.* No. WPS 4901. Washington, DC: World Bank.

Dastgheib, A., J. Reyns, S. Thammasittirong, S. Weesakul, M. Thatcher, and R. Ranasinghe. 2016. Variations in the Wave Climate and Sediment Transport Due to Climate Change along the Coast of Vietnam. *Journal of Marine Science and Engineering.* 4 (4). 86.

Deser, C., A. S. Phillips, M. A. Alexander, and B. V. Smoliak. 2014. Projecting North American Climate over the Next 50 Years: Uncertainty Due to Internal Variability. *Journal of Climate.* 27 (6). pp. 2271–2296.

Duc, D. M., K. Yasuhara, N. M. Hieu, and N. C. Lan. 2017. Climate Change Impacts on a Large-Scale Erosion Coast of Hai Hau District, Vietnam and the Adaptation. *Journal of Coastal Conservation.* 21 (1). pp. 47–62.

Erban, L. E., S. M. Gorelick, and H. A. Zebker. 2014. Groundwater Extraction, Land Subsidence, and Sea-Level Rise in the Mekong Delta, Vietnam. *Environmental Research Letters.* 9 (8). 084010.

Flato, G., J. Marotzke, B. Abiodun, P. Braconnot, S. C. Chou, W. Collins, P. Cox, F. Driouech, S. Emori, V. Eyring, C. Forest, P. Gleckler, E. Guilyardi, C. Jakob, V. Kattsov, C. Reason, and M. Rummukainen. 2013. Evaluation of Climate Models. In: Stocker, T. F., D. Qin, G.-K. Plattner, M. Tignor, S. K. Allen, J. Boschung, A. Nauels, Y. Xia, V. Bex, and P. M. Midgley, eds. *Climate Change 2013: The Physical Science Basis; Contribution of Working Group I to the Fifth Assessment Report of the Intergovernmental Panel on Climate Change.* Cambridge University Press.

Fowler, H. J., and C. G. Kilsby. 2003. A Regional Frequency Analysis of United Kingdom Extreme Rainfall from 1961 to 2000. *International Journal of Climatology.* 23 (11). pp. 1313–1334.

Fowler, H. J., S. Blenkinsop, and C. Tebaldi. 2007. Linking Climate Change Modelling to Impacts Studies: Recent Advances in Downscaling Techniques for Hydrological Modelling. *International Journal of Climatology.* 27 (12). pp. 1547–1578.

Guerreiro, S. B., H. J. Fowler, R. Barbero, S. Westra, G. Lenderink, S. Blenkinsop, E. Lewis, and X.-F. Li. 2018. Detection of Continental-Scale Intensification of Hourly Rainfall Extremes. *Nature Climate Change.* 8 (9). pp. 803–807.

Hallegatte, S. 2009. Strategies to Adapt to an Uncertain Climate Change. *Global Environmental Change.* 19 (2). pp. 240–247.

Hallegatte, S., C. Green, R. J. Nicholls, and J. Corfee-Morlot. 2013. Future Flood Losses in Major Coastal Cities. *Nature Climate Change.* 3. pp. 802–806.

Hanh, P. T. T., and M. Furukawa. 2007. Impact of Sea Level Rise on Coastal Zone of Vietnam. *Bulletin of College of Science, University of the Ryukyus.* 84. pp. 45–59.

Hawkins, E., and R. Sutton. 2010. The Potential to Narrow Uncertainty in Projections of Regional Precipitation Change. *Climate Dynamics.* 37 (1–2). pp. 407–418.

Healy, T. 1996. Sea Level Rise and Impacts on Nearshore Sedimentation: An Overview. *Geologische Rundschau.* 85 (3). pp. 546–553.

Institution of Civil Engineers (ICE). 2015. *Civil Engineering Procedure, Seventh Edition.* London. https://www.icevirtuallibrary.com/doi/book/10.1680/cep.60692.

Intergovernmental Panel on Climate Change (IPCC). 2012. *Managing the Risks of Extreme Events and Disasters to Advance Climate Change Adaptation: A Special Report of Working Groups I and II of the IPCC.* Field, C. B., V. Barros, T. F. Stocker, D. Qin, D. J. Dokken, K. L. Ebi, M. D. Mastrandrea, K. J. Mach, G.-K. Plattner, S. K. Allen, M. Tignor, and P. M. Midgley, eds. Cambridge University Press.

Katsman, C. A., A. Sterl, J. J. Beersma, H. W. van den Brink, J. A. Church, W. Hazeleger, R. E. Kopp, D. Kroon, J. Kwadijk, R. Lammersen, J. Lowe, M. Oppenheimer, H.-P. Plag, J. Ridley, H. von Storch, D. G. Vaughan, P. Vellinga, L. L. A. Vermeersen, R. S. W. van de Wal, and R. Weisse. 2011. Exploring High-End Scenarios for Local Sea Level Rise to Develop Flood Protection Strategies for a Low-Lying Delta—The Netherlands as an Example. *Climatic Change.* 109 (3–4). pp. 617–645.

Katzfey, J. J., J. L. McGregor, and R. Suppiah. 2014. *High-Resolution Climate Projections for Vietnam: Technical Report.* Commonwealth Scientific and Industrial Research Organisation (CSIRO), Australia.

Kite, G. W. 1988. *Frequency and Risk Analyses in Hydrology.* Fort Collins, Colorado: Water Resources Publications.

Knutson, T. R., J. L. McBride, J. Chan, K. Emanuel, G. Holland, C. Landsea, I. Held, J. P. Kossin, A. K. Srivastava, and M. Sugi. 2010. Tropical Cyclones and Climate Change. *Nature Geoscience.* 3. pp. 157–163.

Knutti, R., R. Furrer, C. Tebaldi, J. Cermak, and G. A. Meehl. 2010. Challenges in Combining Projections from Multiple Climate Models. *Journal of Climate.* 23 (10). pp. 2739–2758.

Kriebel, D. L., and R. G. Dean. 1993. Convolution Method for Time-Dependent Beach-Profile Response. *Journal of Waterway, Port, Coastal, and Ocean Engineering.* 119 (2). pp. 204–226.

Lempert, R. J., D. G. Groves, S. W. Popper, and S. C. Bankes. 2006. A General, Analytic Method for Generating Robust Strategies and Narrative Scenarios. *Management Science.* 52 (4). pp. 514–528.

Lenderink, G., R. Barbero, J. M. Loriaux, and H. J. Fowler. 2017. Super-Clausius-Clapeyron Scaling of Extreme Hourly Convective Precipitation and Its Relation to Large-Scale Atmospheric Conditions. *Journal of Climate*. 30 (15). pp. 6037–6052.

Life Cycle Engineering (LCE). 2015. *Life Cycle Asset Management*. White paper. https://www.lce.com/pdfs/LCAM-Whitepaper-204.pdf.

Lochbihler, K., G. Lenderink, and A. P. Siebesma. 2017. The Spatial Extent of Rainfall Events and Its Relation to Precipitation Scaling. *Geophysical Research Letters*. 44. pp. 8629–8636.

McPhillips, L. E., H. Chang, M. V. Chester, Y. Depietri, E. Friedman, N. B. Grimm, J. S. Kominoski, T. McPhearson, P. Méndez-Lázaro, E. J. Rosi, and J. Shafiei Shiva. 2018. Defining Extreme Events: A Cross-Disciplinary Review. *Earth's Future*. 6 (3). pp. 441–455.

McSweeney, C. F., R. G. Jones, R. W. Lee, and D. P. Rowell. 2015. Selecting CMIP5 GCMs for Downscaling over Multiple Regions. *Climate Dynamics*. 44 (11–12). pp. 3237–3260.

Meehl, G. A., T. F. Stocker, W. D. Collins, P. Friedlingstein, A. T. Gaye, J. M. Gregory, A. Kitoh, R. Knutti, J. M. Murphy, A. Noda, S. C. B. Raper, I. G. Watterson, A. J. Weaver, and Z.-C. Zhao. 2007. Global Climate Projections. In: Solomon, S., D. Qin, M. Manning, Z. Chen, M. Marquis, K. B. Averyt, M. Tignor, and H. L. Miller, eds. *Climate Change 2007: The Physical Science Basis: Contribution of Working Group I to the Fourth Assessment Report of the Intergovernmental Panel on Climate Change*. Cambridge University Press.

Menabde, M., A. Seed, and G. Pegram. 1999. A Simple Scaling Model for Extreme Rainfall. *Water Resources Research*. 35 (1). pp. 335–339.

Mertz, B., J. C. J. H. Aerts, K. Arnbjerg-Nielsen, M. Baldi, A. Becker, A. Bichet, G. Blöschl, L. M. Bouwer, A. Brauer, F. Cioffi, J. M. Delgado, M. Gocht, F. Guzzetti, S. Harrigan, K. Hirschboeck, C. Kilsby, W. Kron, H.-H. Kwon, U. Lall, R. Merz, K. Nissen, P. Salvatti, T. Swierczynski, U. Ulbrich, A. Viglione, P. J. Ward, M. Weiler, B. Wilhelm, and M. Nied. 2014. Floods and Climate: Emerging Perspectives for Flood Risk Assessment and Management. *Natural Hazards and Earth System Sciences*. 14. pp. 1921–1942.

Milly, P. C. D., R. T. Wetherald, K. A. Dunne, and T. L. Delworth. 2002. Increasing Risk of Great Floods in a Changing Climate. *Nature*. 415 (6871). pp. 514–517.

Minderhoud, P. S. J., G. Erkens, V. H. Pham, V. T. Bui, L. Erban, H. Kooi, and E. Stouthamer. 2017. Impacts of 25 Years of Groundwater Extraction on Subsidence in the Mekong Delta, Vietnam. *Environmental Research Letters*. 12 (6). pp. 1–13. 064006.

Ministry of Agriculture, Fisheries and Food (MAFF), United Kingdom. 2001. *Flood and Coastal Defence Project Appraisal Guidance: Overview*. FCDPAG1. London: HMSO.

Ministry of Natural Resources and Environment (MONRE), Viet Nam. 2016. *Climate Change and Sea Level Rise Scenarios for Viet Nam*. Prepared by the Viet Nam Institute of Meteorology, Hydrology and Climate Change, Ha Noi.

Muis, S., I. D. Haigh, G. G. Nobre, J. C. J. H. Aerts, and P. J. Ward. 2018. Influence of El Niño-Southern Oscillation on Global Coastal Flooding. *Earth's Future*. 6 (9). pp. 1311–1322.

Nagai, K., S. Kono, and D. X. Quang. 1998. *Coastal Engineering Journal*. 40 (4). pp. 347–366.

Neumann, J. E., K. A. Emanuel, S. Ravela, L. C. Ludwig, and C. Verly. 2015. Risks of Coastal Storm Surge and the Effect of Sea Level Rise in the Red River Delta, Vietnam. *Sustainability*. 7. pp. 6553–6572.

Nicholls, R. J., N. Marinova, J. A. Lowe, S. Brown, P. Vellinga, D. de Gusmão, J. Hinkel, and R. S. J. Tol. 2011. Sea-Level Rise and Its Possible Impacts Given a 'Beyond 4°C World' in the Twenty-First Century. *Philosophical Transactions of the Royal Society of London, A*. 369. pp. 161–181.

Nicholls, R. J., S. E. Hanson, J. A. Lowe, R. A. Warrick, X. Lu, and A. J. Long. 2014. Sea Level Scenarios for Evaluating Coastal Impacts. *WIREs Climate Change*. 5 (1). pp. 129–150.

Osinowo, A., X. Lin, D. Zhao, Z. Wang, and E. Ferrero. 2016. *Advances in Meteorology*. 2016. pp. 1–21. Article ID 2419353.

Pilkey, O. H., R. S. Young, S. R. Riggs, A. W. S. Smith, H. Wu, and W. D. Pilkey. 1993. The Concept of Shoreface Profile of Equilibrium: A Critical Review. *Journal of Coastal Research*. 9 (1). pp. 255–278.

Pol, T. D., and J. Hinkel. 2019. Uncertainty Representations of Mean Sea-Level Change: A Telephone Game? *Climatic Change*. 152 (3). pp. 393–411.

Pruszak, Z., M. Szmytkiewicz, N. M. Hung, and P. van Ninh. 2002. Coastal Processes in the Red River Delta Area, Vietnam. *Coastal Engineering Journal*. 44 (2). pp. 97–126.

Racherla, P. N., D. T. Shindell, and G. S. Faluvegi. 2012. The Added Value to Global Model Projections of Climate Change by Dynamical Downscaling: A Case Study over the Continental U.S. Using the GISS-ModelE2 and WRF Models. *Journal of Geophysical Research: Atmospheres*. 117. D20118.

Ranger, N. T. Reeder, and J. Lowe. 2013. Addressing 'Deep' Uncertainty over Long-Term Climate in Major Infrastructure Projects: Four Innovations of the Thames Estuary 2100 Project. *EURO Journal on Decision Processes*. 1 (3). pp. 233–262.

Rosenzweig, C., W. D. Solecki, R. Blake, M. Bowman, C. Faris, V. Gornitz, R. Horton, K. Jacob, A. LeBlanc, R. Leichenko, M. Linkin, D. Major, M. O'Grady, L. Patrick, E. Sussman, G. Yohe, and R. Zimmerman. 2011. Developing Coastal Adaptation to Climate Change in the New York City Infrastructure-Shed: Process, Approach, Tools, and Strategies. *Climatic Change*. 106 (1). pp. 93–127.

Schimanski, A., and K. Stattegger. 2005. Deglacial and Holocene Evolution of the Vietnam Shelf: Stratigraphy, Sediments and Sea-Level Change. *Marine Geology*. 214 (4). pp. 365–387.

Schroeer, K., and G. Kirchengast. 2018. Sensitivity of Extreme Precipitation to Temperature: The Variability of Scaling Factors from a Regional to Local Perspective. *Climate Dynamics*. 50 (11–12). pp. 3981–3994.

Slangen, A. B. A., M. Carson, C. A. Katsman, R. S. W. Van de Wal, A. Köhl, L. L. A. Vermeersen, and D. Stammer. 2014. Projecting Twenty-First Century Regional Sea-Level Changes. *Climatic Change.* 124 (1–2). pp. 317–332.

Smajgl, A., T. Q. Toan, D. K. Nhan, J. Ward, N. H. Trung, L. Q. Tri, V. P. D. Tri, and P. T. Vu. 2015. Responding to Rising Sea Levels in the Mekong Delta. *Nature Climate Change.* 5. pp. 167–174.

Smith, K. A., R. L. Wilby, C. Broderick, C. Prudhomme, T. Matthews, S. Harrigan, and C. Murphy. 2018. Navigating Cascades of Uncertainty—As Easy as ABC? Not Quite…. *Journal of Extreme Events.* 5 (1). 1850007.

Solomon, S., G.-K. Plattner, R. Knutti, and P. Friedlingstein. 2009. Irreversible Climate Change Due to Carbon Dioxide Emissions. *Proceedings of the National Academy of Sciences of the United States of America.* 106 (6). pp. 1704–1709.

Su, H.-T., and Y.-K. Tung. 2013. Incorporating Uncertainty of Distribution Parameters Due to Sampling Errors in Flood-Damage-Reduction Project Evaluation. *Water Resources Research.* 49 (3). pp. 1680–1692.

Sun, F., M. L. Roderick, and G. D. Farquhar. 2018. Rainfall Statistics, Stationarity, and Climate Change. *Proceedings of the National Academy of Sciences of the United States of America.* 115 (10). pp. 2305–2310.

Taylor, K. E., R. J. Stouffer, and G. A. Meehl. 2012. An Overview of CMIP5 and the Experiment Design. *Bulletin of the American Meteorological Society.* 93 (4). pp. 485–498.

Thai, T. H., N. B. Thuy, V. H. Dang, S. Kim, and L. R. Hole. 2017. Impact of the Interaction of Surge, Wave and Tide on a Storm Surge on the North Coast of Vietnam. *Procedia IUTAM.* 25. pp. 82–91.

Thao, N. D., H. Takagi, and M. Esteban, ed. 2014. *Coastal Disasters and Climate Change in Vietnam: Engineering and Planning Perspectives.* Amsterdam: Elsevier.

Thuc, T., and D. H. Son. 2012. Tidal Regime along Vietnam Coast under Impacts of Sea Level Rise. *Journal of Science: Earth Sciences.* 28. pp. 133–139.

Thuy, N. B., S. Kim, D. D. Chien, V. H. Dang, H. D. Cuong, C. Wettre, and L. R. Hole. 2017. Assessment of Storm Surge along the Coast of Central Vietnam. *Journal of Coastal Research.* 33 (3). pp. 518–530.

Tien, P. H., and N. Van Cu. 2005. *Forecasting the Erosion and Sedimentation in the Coastal and River Mouth Areas and Preventive Measures.* State Level Research Project, Hanoi. 497 pp.

Tran, N. N., K. Nagai, H. Kubota, N. N. Hue, and D. X. Quang. 2004. Statistical Characteristics of Unusual Waves Observed at Danang, Vietnam. In: Goda, Y., W. Kioka, and K. Nadaoka, eds. *Asian and Pacific Coasts 2003: Proceedings of the 2nd International Conference.* Singapore: World Scientific Publishing.

Veijalainen, N., and B. Vehviläinen, B. 2008. The Effect of Climate Change on Design Floods of High Hazard Dams in Finland. *Hydrology Research.* 39 (5–6). pp. 465–477.

Wang, C., J. Liang, and K. I. Hodges. 2017. Projections of Tropical Cyclones Affecting Vietnam under Climate Change: downscaled HadGEM2-ES Using PRECIS 2.1. *Quarterly Journal of the Royal Meteorological Society.* 143 (705). pp. 1,844–1,859.

Wilby, R. L., R. J. Nicholls, R. Warren, H. S. Wheater, D. Clarke, and R. J. Dawson. 2011. Keeping Nuclear and Other Coastal Sites Safe from Climate Change. *Proceedings of the Institution of Civil Engineers: Civil Engineering.* 164 (3). pp. 129–136.

Wilby, R. L., and T. M. L. Wigley. 2002. Future Changes in the Distribution of Daily Precipitation Totals across North America. *Geophysical Research Letters.* 29 (7). 39-1. 10.1029/2001GL013048.

Wilks, D. S. 1995. *Statistical Methods in the Atmospheric Sciences.* Vol. 59, International Geophysics Series. San Diego, California: Academic Press.

Yin, J., D. Yu, and R. L. Wilby. 2015. Modelling the Impact of Land Subsidence on Urban Pluvial Flooding: A Case Study of Downtown Shanghai, China. *Science of the Total Environment.* 544. pp. 744–753.

Yun, K. S., S. W. Yeh, and K. H. Ha. 2016. Inter-El Niño Variability in CMIP5 Models: Model Deficiencies and Future Changes. *Journal of Geophysical Research: Atmospheres.* 121 (8). pp. 3,894–3,906.

Further Reading

Climate Change Adjustments for Project Design

Broderick, C., C. Murphy, R. L. Wilby, T. Matthews, C. Prudhomme, and M. Adamson. 2019. Using a Scenario–Neutral Framework to Avoid Potential Maladaptation to Future Flood Risk. *Water Resources Research*. 55 (2). pp. 1079–1104.

Commonwealth Scientific and Industrial Research Organisation (CSIRO) and Australian Bureau of Meteorology (ABOM). 2015. *Climate Change in Australia Information for Australia's Natural Resource Management Regions: Technical Report*. Melbourne: CSIRO and ABOM. https://www.climatechangeinaustralia.gov.au/en/publications-library/technical-report/ (accessed 27 August 2018).

Environment Agency, UK. 2016. *Adapting to Climate Change: Advice for Flood and Coastal Erosion Risk Management Authorities*. Bristol. https://www.gov.uk/government/publications/adapting-to-Climate change-for-risk-management-authorities (accessed 27 August 2018).

International Hydropower Association (IHA). 2019. *Hydropower Sector Climate Resilience Guide*. London. https://www.hydropower.org/publications/hydropower-sector-climate-resilience-guide.

International Organization for Standardization (ISO). 2018. *Adaptation to Climate Change—Principles, Requirements and Guidelines*. ISO 14090. https://www.iso.org/obp/ui/#iso:std:iso:14090:dis:ed-1:v1:en (accessed 27 August 2018).

Kuklicke, C., and D. Demeritt. 2016. Adaptive and Risk-Based Approaches to Climate Change and the Management of Uncertainty and Institutional Risk: The Case of Future Flooding in England. *Global Environmental Change*. 37. pp. 56–68.

Netherlands Ministry of Infrastructure and Environment. 2014. *Guideline for Stress Testing the Climate Resilience of Urban Areas*. Prepared by F. van de Ven, J. Buma, and T. Vos. https://climate-adapt.eea.europa.eu/metadata/guidances/guideline-for-stress-testing-the-climate-resilience-of-urban-areas/11258895 (accessed 27 August 2018).

New York City Panel on Climate Change (NPCC). 2013. *Climate Risk Information 2013: Observations, Climate Change Projections, and Maps*. C. Rosenzweig and W. Solecki, eds., NPCC2. Prepared for use by the City of New York Special Initiative on Rebuilding and Resiliency.

United States Army Corps of Engineers. 2019. *Incorporating Sea Level Change in Civil Works ER 1110-2-8162. Sea Level Change Calculator*.

Adjusting Extreme Sub-daily Rainfall Estimates

Alam, M. S., and A. Elshorbagy. 2015. Quantification of the Climate Change-Induced Variations in Intensity–Duration–Frequency Curves in the Canadian Prairies. *Journal of Hydrology*. 527. pp. 990–1005.

Cheng, L., and A. AghaKouchak. 2014. Nonstationary Precipitation Intensity-Duration-Frequency Curves for Infrastructure Design in a Changing Climate. *Scientific Reports*. 4. 7093.

Courty, L. G., R. L. Wilby, J. K. Hillier, and L. J. Slater. 2019. Intensity-Duration-Frequency Curves of Precipitation at the Global Scale. *Environmental Research Letters*. 14 (8). 084045.

De Paola, F., M. Giugni, M. E. Topa, and E. Bucchignani. 2014. Intensity-Duration-Frequency (IDF) Rainfall Curves, for Data Series and Climate Projection in African Cities. *SpringerPlus*. 3. 133.

Fadhel, S., M. A. Rico-Ramirez, and D. Han. 2017. Uncertainty of Intensity–Duration–Frequency (IDF) Curves Due to Varied Climate Baseline Periods. *Journal of Hydrology*. 547. pp. 600–612.

Herath, S. M., P. R. Sarukkalige, and V. T. V. Nguyen. 2016. A Spatial Temporal Downscaling Approach to Development of IDF Relations for Perth Airport Region in the Context of Climate Change. *Hydrological Sciences Journal*. 61 (11). pp. 2061–2070.

Kuok, K. K. K., D. Y. S. Mah, M. A. Imteaz, and S. M. Kueh. 2016. Comparison of Future Intensity Duration Frequency Curve by Considering the Impact of Climate Change: Case Study for Kuching City. *International Journal of River Basin Management*. 14 (1). pp. 47–55.

Li, J., F. Johnson, J. Evans, and A. Sharma. 2017. A Comparison of Methods to Estimate Future Sub-daily Design Rainfall. *Advances in Water Resources*. 110. pp. 215–227.

Lima, C. H. R., H. H. Kwon, and J. Y. Kim. 2016. A Bayesian Beta Distribution Model for Estimating Rainfall IDF Curves in a Changing Climate. *Journal of Hydrology*. 540. pp. 744–756.

So, B. J., J. Y. Kim, H. H. Kwon, and C. H. R. Lima. 2017. Stochastic Extreme Downscaling Model for an Assessment of Changes in Rainfall Intensity-Duration-Frequency Curves over South Korea Using Multiple Regional Climate Models. *Journal of Hydrology*. 553. pp. 321–337.

Tfwala, C. M., L. D. van Rensburg, R. Schall, S. M. Mosia, and P. Dlamini. 2017. Precipitation Intensity-Duration-Frequency Curves and Their Uncertainties for Ghaap Plateau. *Climate Risk Management*. 16. pp. 1–9.

Policy and Practice of Adaptation in the Coastal Zone

Adger, W. N. 1999. Social Vulnerability to Climate Change and Extremes in Coastal Vietnam. *World Development*. 27 (2). pp. 249–269.

Adger, W. N., N. W. Arnell, and E. L. Tompkins. 2005. Successful Adaptation to Climate Change across Scales. *Global Environmental Change*. 15 (2). pp. 77–86.

Bao, T. Q. 2011. Effect of Mangrove Forest Structures on Wave Attenuation in Coastal Vietnam. *Oceanologia*. 53 (3). pp. 807–818.

Danh, V. T., and S. Mushtaq. 2011. Living with Floods: An Evaluation of the Resettlement Program of the Mekong Delta of Vietnam. In: Stewart, M. A., and P. A. Coclanis, eds. *Environmental Change and Agricultural Sustainability in the Mekong Delta*. Advances in Global Change Research Series 45. Dordrecht: Springer. pp. 181–204.

Das, S., and J. R. Vincent. 2009. Mangroves Protected Villages and Reduced Death Toll during Indian Super Cyclone. *Proceedings of the National Academy of Sciences of the United States of America*. 106 (18). pp. 7357–7360.

Gedan, K. B., M. L. Kirwan, E. Wolanski, E. B. Barbier, and B. R. Silliman. 2010. The Present and Future Role of Coastal Wetland Vegetation in Protecting Shorelines: Answering Recent Challenges to the Paradigm. *Climatic Change*. 106 (1). pp. 7–29.

Mazda, Y., M. Magi, M. Kogo, and P. N. Hong. 1997. Mangroves as a Coastal Protection from Waves in the Tong King Delta, Vietnam. *Mangroves and Salt Marshes*. 1 (2). pp. 127–135.

Stive, M. J. F., L. O. Fresco, P. Kabat, B. W. A. H. Parmet, and C. P. Veerman. 2011. How the Dutch Plan to Stay Dry over the Next Century. *Proceedings of the Institution of Civil Engineers: Civil Engineering*. 164 (3). pp. 114–121.

Tu, T. T., and V. Nitivattananon. 2011. Adaptation to Flood Risks in Ho Chi Minh City, Vietnam. *International Journal of Climate Change Strategies and Management*. 3 (1). pp. 61–73.

Wilby, R. L., and R. Keenan. 2012. Adapting to Flood Risk under Climate Change. *Progress in Physical Geography: Earth and Environment*. 36 (3). pp. 348–378.